# HOW LIBRARIES MUST COMPLY WITH THE AMERICANS WITH DISABILITIES ACT (ADA)

# HOW LIBRARIES MUST COMPLY WITH THE AMERICANS WITH DISABILITIES ACT (ADA)

Compiled and edited by
*Donald D. Foos and Nancy C. Pack*

ORYX PRESS
1992

Copyright © 1992 by The Oryx Press
4041 North Central at Indian School Road
Phoenix, Arizona 85012-3397

Published simultaneously in Canada

Printed and Bound in the United States of America

∞ The paper used in this publication meets the minimum requirements of American National Standard for Information Science—Permanence of Paper for Printed Library Materials, ANSI Z39.48, 1984.

**Library of Congress Cataloging-in-Publication Data**

How libraries must comply with the Americans with Disabilities Act (ADA) / compiled and edited by Donald D. Foos and Nancy C. Pack; foreword by Gerald Jahoda.
    p.  cm.
Includes bibliographical references and index.
ISBN 0-89774-760-7
    1. Libraries and the handicapped—United States.  2. Handicapped—Legal status, laws, etc.—United States.  I. Foos, Donald D.
II. Pack, Nancy C.
Z711.92.H3H68  1992
027.6'63—dc20                            92-3796
                                                      CIP

# Contents

# Foreword

GERALD JAHODA

Blind or visually disabled persons, like myself, now have to use most libraries by means of an attendant. When I use a library to do a literature search, my attendant searches the catalog, the periodical indexes, and other bibliographic tools under headings given to him or her, reads entries aloud so that I can select potentially relevant publications, and then retrieves these publications from the stacks. Persons with other types of disabilities may also have to use libraries through attendants or face other barriers to library use. Persons in wheelchairs may face physical barriers in entering the library and moving from place to place in the library. Deaf persons may be faced with communication barriers that prevent them from describing their information needs. This may be because the library staff does not know how to communicate with deaf persons or because the library does not have a telephone device for the deaf.

These and other barriers to library service to disabled persons will need to be removed so that the estimated 43 million disabled Americans have access to library service equal to that of nondisabled persons. That, in effect, is the message of the Americans with Disabilities Act of 1990 (ADA), which is now the law of the land.

The language of the law, while sometimes majestic and awe inspiring, is often difficult for the layperson to understand. The authors of this publication, five well-known librarians and a lawyer who now works with disabled college students, have made the effort of studying the ADA as it applies to libraries. Their thoughtful and informative essays should be read by library administrators of public, academic, school, and special libraries.

While the use of technology is only part of the answer to the problem of making library service accessible to disabled persons, much progress has been made along these lines. Computer technology, telecommunication technology, and bibliographic databases, the full texts of books, and other types of publications in machine readable form are making possible equal access to library service by disabled persons. A blind or visually disabled person, a person in a wheelchair, or a deaf person may now have access to a significant segment of recorded knowledge from a computer located either in the library or at his or her home. With appropriate adaptive devices, one may search by oneself catalogs and indexes to periodicals, as well as other bibliographic tools, and make relevance judgments based on abstracts or bibliographic data given in the entry. In some periodical indexes, the full text of the cited publication may either be read at the computer or ordered electronically. This library-use scenario is made possible by commercially available adaptive computer input and output devices. Examples of such devices are braille input and output devices, screen character enlargement programs, speech synthesizers, page scanners that convert printed text into machine readable form, and keyboards that may be accessed by persons with limited use of their hands.

Librarianship shares many characteristics with other professions, including the gap between what is and what should be in the way of professional service. Another shared characteristic is the profession's attempt to close this gap so that service is continuously improved and offered to as large a segment of the population as possible. During my 40 years in the library profession, I have seen library service to other minority groups initiated, imported, and expanded despite the ever-present shortage of funds, resources, and personnel. I am convinced that the library profession will also meet the challenge of providing equal access to library service to persons with disabilities. Not only is this the law of the land, it is the right thing to do.

# Preface

On July 26, 1990, 2,000 disability rights activists witnessed President George Bush signing the Americans with Disabilities Act of 1990 (ADA) into law.[1] With this important piece of legislation, "43 million people with disabilities were welcomed to full citizenship by the President of the United States."[2] The ADA recognizes people with disabilities as a class; "it elevates that class by affording protections equal to those afforded race and gender minorities; and it establishes in the law of the land the principle of equal opportunity for people who are disabled."[3]

Representative Steny Hoyer of Maryland, chief sponsor of the bill in the U.S. House of Representatives, was the original cosponsor of the ADA each time it was introduced. After former Representative Tony Coelho of California, the other original cosponsor, left Congress, Hoyer took over shepherding the ADA through the House. He considered the ADA to be a "major civil rights bill."[4] The Democratic leadership listed the ADA "as a major legislative priority of the year and gave it special attention."[5] More than 250 of the 435 members of the House were listed as cosponsors of the ADA.

The legislative history of the Americans with Disabilities Act of 1990 is as follows: Senate Bill 933 (S933) was considered and passed on September 7, 1989. House Bill 2273 was considered on May 17, 1990 and passed on May 22; S933 passed in lieu. The Senate recommitted the Conference Report on July 11, 1990; the House agreed to the Conference Report, and on July 13 the Senate agreed to the Conference Report. The ADA became Public Law 101-336 with President Bush's signature on July 26, 1990.

In an open letter to the Friends of the Disability Rights Education and Defense Fund (DREDF), executive director Mary Lou Breslin commented as follows on the ADA:

For eleven years, we who worked at DREDF have devoted ourselves to the dream of the full integration of people with disabilities into the life of this country. When President Bush signed the Americans with Disabilities Act, we knew our efforts were worthwhile . . . .

The ADA has been called a milestone and a landmark. It is all of that, and a turning point in the history of the United States, from which we will never look back and never back down. The ADA brings the dream within reach, as it makes a promise of real equality . . . .

We believe that great vigilance is necessary. First—all of us must understand our rights under the law, to ensure their enforcement. Second—the all-important regulations which spell out those rights must conform to the intent of the [ADA] and not weaken its purpose and effect. . . .[6]

The Americans with Disabilities Act of 1990 directs public and private libraries—academic, public, school, and special—to provide services to people with disabilities that are equal to services provided to citizens without disabilities. The existence of the ADA and its regulations and the projected vigilant pursuit of equal services by consumers with disabilities will require librarians to inform themselves about methods to meet the needs for library services of people with disabilities.

The ADA, in its broadest definition, is landmark legislation that extends civil rights protection to people with disabilities. These rights include equal access to:

- Employment
- Public Services and Accommodations
- Transportation
- Telecommunications Relay

The ADA differs from Section 504 of the Rehabilitation Act of 1973 in that it specifies how people with disabilities will be able to access information, programs, and resources contained in the library building. The ADA also redefines employment, transportation, and telecommunication regulations. The ADA affects libraries both as employers and as service-providers.

As employers, libraries must make reasonable efforts to accommodate the disabilities of qualified applicants and employees. Providing accommodations under the ADA is unnecessary if employers can prove that to do so would impose unreasonable and undue hardship on the library operations.

Providing people with disabilities with the same services offered to people without disabilities means equal access to information, programs, and resources. If the library does not comply with the ADA as an employer or service-provider, remedies are the same as under Title VII of the Civil Rights Act of 1964; individuals may bring private lawsuits to obtain court orders to stop discrimination. Individuals can also file complaints with the U.S. Attorney General, who may file lawsuits to stop discrimination and obtain monetary damages and penalties.

Now that the ADA is law and its regulations mandate equal access to services and programs provided by libraries, local pressures will greatly influence library managers/administrators to fully understand the applications of the ADA and its regulations as they relate to their respective library situations. Advocacy and vigilant consumer groups will use the ADA to encourage equal access to services for their particular consumer group. Library employees with disabilities will be requesting adaptations to the library work and public space as required by the new law. And, as public transportation and telephone communication access are provided to them under the ADA, people with disabilities will place increasing demands on libraries for the same services provided to those without disabilities in their service community.

Library managers/administrators and staff members of libraries, responding to these pressures, will be in need of information and strategies to make their services and materials accessible. This book is designed to assist in meeting these responsibilities.

In Chapter 1, "Libraries and the Americans with Disabilities Act," Michael Gunde interprets and explains the Act from the point of view of a practicing library administrator with extensive experience working with people with disabilities. He provides background data on people with disabilities and describes the nation's goals regarding such individuals. Mr. Gunde discusses the parts of the Act that concern employment, public services, and public accommodations and services provided by private entities. He cites specific sections of the Act and its regulations throughout the chapter.

In Chapter 2, "Planning to Implement the ADA in the Library," Ruth O'Donnell uses an excellent six-step ADA planning model as a guide that users of this publication may follow to plan for ADA compliance. She accompanies each step with lists of important information resources located at the end of the chapter. Organizations, books, articles, pamphlets, reports, video resources, advocacy groups, service providers, federal and state agencies, publications (free and for-sale), and computerized databases are found throughout the five lists, with names, addresses, telephone numbers (Voice, TDD, FAX, and electronic bulletin boards), and other pertinent information on the ADA. Ms. O'Donnell provides annotated bibliographic entries for publications included in the five lists and in the chapter.

O'Donnell also describes fully assistive devices—auxiliary aids and services that are used to overcome visual, hearing, speech, and physical limitations. In discussing the library's self-evaluation, she includes the utilization of public forums, advocacy groups, library consumers, advisory committees, task forces, and the identification of, and communication with, people with disabilities. Self-evaluation methods and questions as related to building and facilities access, service access, policies and procedures, staff training, and the library's employment practices are included in this chapter.

Marilyn Karrenbrock, in Chapter 3, "The Impact of the ADA Upon School Library Media Centers," develops a historical perspective on legislation affecting the education of children with disabilities, beginning with the first federal law on the subject—Public Law 19-8, which in 1828 provided assistance for the establishment of a school for the deaf in Kentucky—and ending with the Americans with Disabilities Act of 1990. She states that if previous laws, such as Public Law 94-142, the Education for All Handicapped Children Act of 1975, have been widely and effectively implemented, the ADA should have little direct impact upon school library media centers. Karrenbrock suggests that the ADA may have indirect effects upon school library media centers and that media specialists should take advantage of the new opportunities and possibilities that the law provides.

Karrenbrock also compares Section 504 of the Rehabilitation Act of 1973 with the Americans with Disabilities Act and addresses several situations where the ADA may have a direct impact on school library media centers.

In Chapter 4, "The Americans with Disabilities Act: The Legal Implications," Peter Manheimer states that the ADA is not intended to provide special privileges and, unlike Sections 501 and 503 of the Rehabilitation Act of 1973, is not an affirmative action statute. Utilizing his legal education and his extensive experience as a practicing attorney in Florida, Manheimer dissects the ADA from a legal point of view and applies it to library operations and situations. Mr. Manheimer asks many questions about how ADA compliance will apply to libraries. In doing so, he provides many possible answers to these questions. Employment, specifically job requirements, essential functions, reasonable accommodations in job functions, undue hardship, and disability inquiries are just a few of the topics included in this chapter.

Chapter 5, "ADA Case Studies and Exercises," offers a series of ADA case studies developed by Don Foos and Nancy Pack. These case studies are purely hypothetical and theoretical in nature, but are based on the ADA and its regulations and guidelines, and presented as possible or probable actual situations. Readers will find these case studies useful as graphic illustrations of the law and its application. Because the ADA has not been tested in the courts, and since all libraries will have to be in compliance, these case studies are presented as examples of what could happen in your library.

Chapter 6, "Problem Areas and A Quick Guide to the ADA" was developed by Don Foos and Nancy Pack to provide insight into the extensiveness of the ADA. It serves as a companion to the case studies and exercises in Chapter 5.

Four appendixes condense important information on the ADA and related statutes and services. Appendix A explains how to get copies of the ADA and its regulations and guidelines. Appendix B is a quick guide to important ADA deadlines. Appendix C provides a brief description of the National Library Service for the Blind and Physically Handicapped. Appendix D briefly describes the aims of other disability legislation passed prior to the ADA.

Some readers may believe that compliance under Section 504 of the Rehabilitation Act of 1973 will be sufficient to comply under the ADA. This may be the case, but all library managers/administrators are strongly urged to read the Americans with Disabilities Act of 1990 and its regulations and guidelines.

The contributors to this book have provided their interpretations of the ADA as it relates to all types of libraries (Gunde); how the ADA may be implemented in libraries (O'Donnell); the impact of the ADA on school library media centers (Karrenbrock); the legal implications for libraries under the ADA (Manheimer); and ADA case studies, exercises, and problem areas (Foos and Pack). Because this is a first-of-its-kind publication, the contributors have had to rely on their education and personal work experiences as they related to providing library and related services to people with disabilities. In their work experiences, the contributors all have first-hand knowledge of past and present real and implied discriminations against people with disabilities in their workplaces.

President Bush alluded to the fall of the Berlin Wall when he said, "And now I sign legislation which takes a sledgehammer to another wall, one which has, for too many generations, separated Americans with disabilities from the freedom they could glimpse but not grasp. Once again, we rejoice as this barrier falls, proclaiming together we will not accept, we will not excuse, we will not tolerate discrimination in America."[7]

## REFERENCES

1. "July 26, 1990: The Day We've Been Waiting For: Interview with Rep. Steny Hoyer," Disability Rights & Defense Fund (DREDF) *News* (October 1990): 1.

2. Ibid.

3. Ibid.

4. Ibid.

5. Ibid.

6. Ibid, 3.

7. ADA-Texas, *Taking Care of Business* (Austin, TX: Texas Rehabilitation Center, 1991), unpaged.

# Acknowledgments

Appreciation is extended to Donald John Weber, the chief of the Florida Bureau of Library Services for the Blind and Physically Handicapped, for his continuing encouragement to compile this publication on the Americans with Disabilities Act of 1990 and its rules and regulations, and, for his continued assistance and guidance during the compilation of this work. Special appreciation is extended to Debra J. Sears, a library services supervisor in the Information Center of the State Library of Florida, for her endless assistance in providing reference materials, citations, and online computer searches that provided so much information for this publication. Also, appreciation is extended to the reference staff of the Leon County (Tallahassee, Florida) Public Library for their excellent telephone reference service in providing sources for information. The most appreciated are the contributors—Mike Gunde, Ruth O'Donnell, Marilyn H. Karrenbrock, and Peter Manheimer—whose excellent contributions made this publication a reality. A note of appreciation is also extended to Art Stickney, the director of editorial development of the Oryx Press, for his guidance and assistance during the developmental process, and to John Wagner, our editor at the Oryx Press, for his painstaking editorial detail to the finished product.

# Editor and Contributor Profiles

## EDITORS

**Donald D. Foos**, now on long-term disability leave as director of library and information science programs, and director of the Center for Library and Information Science Education and Research (CLISER) from the University of Arkansas at Little Rock, was formerly dean of the Louisiana State University Graduate School of Library Science. He is currently a volunteer consultant with the Florida Bureau of Library Services for the Blind and Physically Handicapped. Previous experience includes work in public and state library agencies in Alabama, Kentucky, Texas, and West Virginia; and also as a faculty member at library schools in Kentucky and New York. Dr. Foos received his master's and advanced master's degrees and doctorate in library science from Florida State University. He is a disabled veteran, serving previously with the U.S. Air Force. Dr. Foos served as a senior instructor and technician in aeromedical evacuation with the USAF School of Aviation Medicine, Air University, U.S. Air Force, and with the 9th Aeromedical Evacuation Squadron in Tachikawa, Japan.

**Nancy C. Pack**, formerly a public library director in Arkansas, is currently a consultant with the Florida Bureau of Library Services for the Blind and Physically Handicapped in the Division of Blind Services of the Florida Department of Education. Her work activities and research are in the area of deposit collections (which includes braille materials, talking books and equipment) in facilities throughout Florida. Dr. Pack received her master's degree in library and information science from the University of Tennessee, and certificates in gerontology and in aging and vision-loss and a doctorate in library and information studies from Florida State University. Her publications are in the areas of deposit collections and services for the blind. Dr. Pack is chairperson of ASCLA's Library Services to the Blind and Physically

Handicapped Forum Program Committee for 1992 and has planned programs about the Americans with Disabilities Act and library services to older adults for American Library Association conferences.

## CONTRIBUTORS

**Michael G. Gunde**, associate library director for the Florida Bureau of Library Services for the Blind and Physically Handicapped, has been involved in giving presentations on the Americans with Disabilities Act of 1990 (ADA) throughout the United States, most recently for the Northern Conference of Librarians for the Blind and Physically Handicapped in Philadelphia. His first published work on the ADA appeared in *American Libraries* (1991)22:806-09, and his Q&A column on the ADA appeared in *Library Journal* in December 1991 116:99. Mr. Gunde received his master's degree in library science from Florida State University. He is editor of *DIKTA*, the publication of the Southern Conference of Librarians for the Blind and Physically Handicapped; he also serves as the chairperson of ALA's Francis Joseph Campbell Award Committee, and as secretary of ASCLA's Libraries Serving Special Populations Committee. Mr. Gunde has also served as a member of the State Library of Florida's Access Task Force on the Americans with Disabilities Act of 1990.

**Gerald Jahoda**, a native of Vienna, is professor emeritus at the School of Library and Information Studies at Florida State University. He is a nationally recognized scholar in the field of information science and documentation and most recently in library service to people with disabilities. Dr. Jahoda holds his master's degree and doctorate in library studies from Columbia University. His professional experience includes work in special libraries in Wisconsin, New Jersey, and New York. Widely published in information science and documentation, Dr. Jahoda is coauthor (with William Needham) of *Improving Library Service to Physically Disabled Persons: A Self-evaluation Checklist* (Libraries Unlimited, 1983). He recently served as a member of the advisory committee for the blind for the Florida Bureau of Library Services for the Blind and Physically Handicapped.

**Marilyn H. Karrenbrock**, associate professor at the Graduate School of Library and Information Science at the University of Tennessee—Knoxville, is coauthor (with Linda Lucas) of *The Disabled Child in the Library: Moving into the Mainstream* (Libraries Unlimited, 1983). Dr. Karrenbrock received her doctorate of education in language education from the University of Georgia, where she also served as a university nonteaching graduate assistant. She also was bibliographer/instructor with the College of Librarianship at the University of South Carolina, where she previously received her master's degree in librarianship. Dr. Karrenbrock has extensive experience as a media specialist in South Carolina and as an elementary education school teacher in California, Louisiana, and Oklahoma. She served as a consultant on library media services for youth with handicaps in school and public library settings at the University of Indiana School of Library and Information Science, and serves as a member of the Tennessee Education Association's State Committee for the Implementation of the *Information Power Standards* in Tennessee.

**Peter Manheimer**, formerly a practicing attorney in Miami, Florida, is currently the assistant coordinator of disabled student services at Florida International University (FIU) in Miami. He also is an adjunct instructor in the Department of Social Science, teaching social environment at Miami Dade Community College. Mr. Manheimer is scheduled to receive the doctorate of education degree in law and political science from FIU in 1992. He holds his J.D. from the University of Miami School of Law. Mr. Manheimer was a delegate to Florida's Governor's Conference on Libraries and Services in 1990, and served as a delegate to the White House Conference on Libraries and Information Services in 1991. He is a wheelchair user, and served on the State Library of Florida's Access Task Force on the Americans with Disabilities Act of 1990, working on issues and recommendations for the director of Florida's Division of Library and Information Service.

**Ruth O'Donnell** is currently the institutions/special clientele consultant with the Bureau of Library Development in the Division of Library and Information Service, Florida Department of State. She formerly served as a special projects coordinator with the Florida Department of Health and Rehabilitative Services. Ms. O'Donnell has extensive work experience as an administrator and residential services director in various residential care facilities in Florida and Connecticut. She has been a library consultant on a self-employed basis and with the Florida State University School of Nursing. Ms. O'Donnell has published on the Americans with Disabilities Act of 1990 and on library services to developmentally disabled persons. She received her master's in library science from Florida State University. Ms. O'Donnell was the chairperson of the State Library of Florida's Access Task Force on the Americans with Disabilities Act of 1990.

# Chapter 1
# Libraries and the Americans with Disabilities Act

## Michael G. Gunde

When President Bush signed the Americans with Disabilities Act (ADA) on July 26, 1990, he established a "clear and comprehensive national mandate for the elimination of discrimination against individuals with disabilities."[1] The American Civil Liberties Union considers the ADA to be "the most important, and perhaps the most complex, piece of civil rights legislation passed in this country in the past 25 years."[2] The ADA addresses discrimination in Employment (Title I), Public Services (Title II), Public Accommodations and Services Operated by Private Entities (Title III), and Telecommunications (Title IV). As noted by former Attorney General Richard Thornburgh, the passage of this landmark legislation "will enable society to benefit from the skills and talents of individuals with disabilities, will allow us all to gain from their individual purchasing power and ability to use it, and will lead to fuller, more productive lives for all Americans."[3]

In drafting the ADA, Congress determined that "some 43,000,000 Americans have one or more physical or mental disabilities, and this number is increasing as the population as a whole is growing older."[4] The Act defines a disability as "a physical or mental impairment that substantially limits one or more of the major life activities . . . [or] a record of such an impairment, or being regarded as having such an impairment."[5] Included in "major life activities" are such functions as "caring for oneself, performing manual tasks, walking, seeing, hearing, speaking, breathing, learning, and working."[6] Since "major life activi-

the general population can perform with little or no difficulty," they also "include, but are not limited to, sitting, standing, lifting, [and] reaching."[7]

Data compiled by the National Institute on Disability and Rehabilitation Research indicate that "more than 20% of all noninstitutionalized persons age 15 and over in the United States have a physical functional limitation (37.3 million people)," including nearly 13 million who have difficulty seeing words in ordinary newsprint and more than 7.5 million who experience problems in hearing what is said in typical conversations.[8] Furthermore, "approximately 1% of the population is estimated to be mentally retarded . . . [which] translates to between 2 and 2.5 million people," while a startling 32.2% of the noninstitutionalized adult population of the United States report having a mental disorder (such as anxiety, antisocial personality, or schizophrenia) during their lifetime.[9] According to the U.S. Department of Education, nearly 950,000 children and youths with mental retardation or severe emotional disturbances were served during the 1989-90 school year.[10] In addition, some 2 million people reside in such institutions as nursing homes and mental hospitals.[11]

The ADA acknowledges that "historically, society has tended to isolate and segregate individuals with disabilities, and despite some improvements, such forms of discrimination against individuals with disabilities continue to be a serious and pervasive social problem."[12] Americans with disabilities form "a discrete and insular minority who have been faced with restrictions and limitations, subjected to a history of purposeful unequal treatment, and relegated to a position of political powerlessness in our society, based on characteristics that are beyond the control of such individuals and resulting from stereotypic assumptions not truly indicative of the ability . . . to participate in, and contribute to society."[13] Furthermore, people with disabilities "continually encounter various forms of discrimination, including outright intentional exclusion, the discriminatory effects of architectural, transportation, and communication barriers, overprotective rules and policies, failure to make modifications to existing facilities and practices, exclusionary qualification standards and criteria, segregation, and relegation to lesser services, programs, activities, benefits, jobs or other opportunities."[14]

According to the ADA, "the Nation's proper goals regarding individuals with disabilities are to assure equality of opportunity, full participation, independent living, and economic self-sufficiency for such individuals."[15] Recognizing that "the continuing existence of unfair and unnecessary discrimination and prejudice denies people with disabilities the opportunity to compete on an equal basis and to pursue those opportunities for which our society is justifiably famous, and costs the United States billions of dollars in unnecessary expenses resulting from dependency and nonproductivity,"[16] the ADA provides "clear, strong, consistent, enforceable standards addressing discrimination against individuals with disabilities."[17] To that end, the ADA ensures "that the Federal Government plays a central role in enforcing the standards established in this Act on behalf of individuals with disabilities"[18] and invokes "the sweep of congressional authority, including the power to enforce the Fourteenth Amendment and to regulate commerce, in order to address the major areas of discrimination faced day-to-day by people with disabilities."[19]

## EMPLOYMENT—TITLE I

The ADA's Title I prohibits discrimination "against a qualified individual with a disability because of the disability of such individual in regard to job application procedures, the hiring, advancement, or discharge of employees, employee compensation, job training, and other terms, conditions, and privileges of employment."[20] A "qualified individual with a disability" is one "who satisfies the requisite skill, experience, education and other job-related requirements of the employment position such individual holds or desires, and who, with or without reasonable accommodation, can perform the essential functions of such position," which are defined as the "fundamental job duties of the employment position the individual with a disability holds or desires."[21]

Employment discrimination against individuals with disabilities is prohibited for private employers with 25 or more workers on July 26, 1992, and for those with 15 or more employees two years later.[22] The U.S. government and corporations wholly owned by it, as well as Native American tribes and bona fide private membership clubs (other than labor organizations) that are exempt from taxation are not covered by the requirements of Title I.[23] Employers that are subdivisions of state or local governments should note that public entities may not discriminate against qualified employees or applicants after January 26, 1992, regardless of the number of persons they employ.[24] In addition, the antidiscrimination provisions of the ADA are explicitly extended to the instrumentalities of the Congress, including the Library of Congress.[25] Church librarians will be interested in knowing that while religious organizations "may require that all applicants and employees conform to the religious tenets" of the church,[26] these organizations "may not discriminate against an individual who satisfies the permitted religious criteria because that individual is disabled."[27]

In its rules to implement Title I of the ADA, the Equal Employment Opportunity Commission (EEOC) explains that a "physical or mental impairment" includes:

> Any physiological disorder, or condition, cosmetic disfigurement, or anatomical loss affecting one or more of the following body systems: neurological, musculoskeletal, special sense organs, respiratory (including speech organs), cardiovascular, reproductive, digestive, genito-urinary, hemic and lymphatic, skin, and endocrine; or any mental or psychological disorder, such as mental illness, and specific learning disabilities.[28]

There are some exceptions to this definition. For example, pregnancy is specifically excluded from coverage as a disability.[29] Likewise, homosexuality and bisexuality are not considered to be "impairments and so are not disabilities" while "transvestism, transsexualism, pedophilia, exhibitionism, voyeurism, gender identity disorders not resulting from physical impairments, or other sexual behavior disorders" as well as "compulsive gambling, kleptomania, or pyromania" and "psychoactive substance abuse disorders resulting from current illegal use of drugs," although presumably mental impairments, are not considered to be disabilities under the ADA definition.[30] However, ADA Title I protects an applicant or employee who

> has successfully completed a supervised drug rehabilitation program and is no longer engaging in the illegal use of drugs, or has otherwise been rehabilitated successfully and is no longer engaging in the illegal use of drugs; or is participating in a supervised rehabilitation program and is no longer engaging in such use; or is erroneously regarded as engaging in such use, but is not engaging in such use.[31]

Elements of discrimination specifically prohibited by Title I of the ADA include "limiting, segregating or classifying a job applicant or employee in a way that adversely affects the opportunities or status of such applicant or employee because of the disability"[32] or "not making reasonable accommodations to the known physical or mental limitation of an otherwise qualified individual" unless the employer "can demonstrate that the accommodation would impose an undue hardship on the operation of the business of such covered entity."[33] It is also a violation for a covered employer to deny "opportunities to a job applicant or employee who is an otherwise qualified individual with a disability" if the denial is the result of "the need of such covered entity to make reasonable accommodation to the physical or mental impairments of the employee or applicant."[34]

Reasonable accommodations in employment include "making existing facilities used by employees readily accessible to and usable by individuals with disabilities,"[35] such as break rooms, cafeterias, and corporate or special libraries provided for use by employees, as well as "job restructuring, part-time or modified work schedules, reassignment to a vacant position, acquisition or modification of equipment or devices, appropriate adjustment or modifications of examinations, training materials or policies, the provision of qualified readers or interpreters, and similar accommodations for individuals with disabilities."[36] The EEOC states in its regulations to implement Title I that the obligation to make reasonable accommodations applies

> to all employment decisions and to the job application process. This obligation does not extend to the provision of adjustments or modifications that are primarily for the personal benefit of the individual with a disability. Thus, if an adjustment or modification is job-related, e.g., specifically assists the individual in performing the duties of a particular job, it will be considered a type of reasonable accommodation. On the other hand, if an adjustment or modification assists the individual throughout his or her daily activities, on and off the job, it will be considered a personal item that the employer is not required to provide. Accordingly, an employer would not be required to provide an employee with a disability with a prosthetic limb, wheelchair, or eyeglasses. Nor would an employer have to provide as an accommodation any amenity or convenience that is not job-related, such as a private hot plate, hot pot, or refrigerator that is not provided to employees without disabilities.[37]

According to the EEOC, in order for an employer to determine what reasonable accommodations are appropriate, "it may be necessary for the covered entity to initiate an informal, interactive process with the qualified individual with a disability" to "identify the precise limitations resulting from the disability and potential reasonable accommodations that could overcome those limitations."[38] This process is necessary to achieve ADA compliance because the needs of each individual with a disability differ; thus it is not possible to produce a checklist of all potentially required accommodations. The EEOC further underscores this point by explaining that many ADA decisions "must be made on a case-by-case basis" and refers to its regulations as "parameters to serve as guidelines in such inquiries."[39]

If an employer believes that the provision of an accommodation constitutes an "undue hardship," which involves "significant difficulty or expense,"[40] factors to be analyzed include the cost and nature of the requested accommodation, the overall fiscal resources of the facility and the covered entity, the number of persons employed, and "the type of operation or operations of the covered entity, including the composition, structure, and functions of the workforce . . . [and] the geographic separateness, administrative, or fiscal relationship of the facility or facilities in question to the covered entity."[41]

Even when an employer can successfully demonstrate that the provision of a specific accommodation would impose an undue hardship, the employer is still "required to provide the accommodation if the funding is available from another source, e.g., a State vocational rehabilitation agency, or if Federal, State or local tax deductions or tax credits are available to offset the cost of the accommodation."[42] Thus, if the employer "receives, or is eligible to receive, monies from an external source that would pay the entire cost of the accommodation, it cannot claim cost as an undue hardship."[43]

The regulations to implement Title I also prohibit an employer from conducting a preemployment medical examination or inquiry as to whether an applicant "is an individual with a disability or as to the nature or severity of such disability," although an employer may ask about "the ability of an applicant to perform job-related functions."[44] However, an employer subject to the provisions of Title I of the ADA may

require a medical examination after an offer of employment has been made to a job applicant and prior to the commencement of the employment duties . . . and may condition an offer of employment on the results . . . if all entering employees are subjected to such an examination regardless of disability [and] information obtained regarding the medical condition or history of the applicant is collected and maintained on separate forms and in separate medical files and is treated as a confidential medical record, except that supervisors and managers may be informed regarding necessary restrictions on the work or duties of the employee and necessary accommodations; first aid and safety personnel may be informed, when appropriate, if the disability might require emergency treatment; and government officials investigating compliance with this Act shall be provided relevant information on request.[45]

In exploring the economic loss to our society caused by employment discrimination against people with disabilities, the EEOC estimates that the implementation of Title I will produce an annual savings of more than $380 million in productivity gains, decreased support payments, and increased taxes paid by workers who received public assistance payments prior to employment. These gains would be only slightly offset by the comparatively low expenditure of less than $17 million for reasonable accommodation costs and less than $25 million for EEOC administrative expenses.[46] A hypothetical example illustrates the long-range benefits of expanding employment opportunities for people with disabilities:

> Take a disabled person who starts work at a $10,000 per annum job. He or she will pay slightly over $2,000 in taxes and will no longer collect $6,000 in [support] benefits. The gain to society is in general at least $8,000 per year for the remainder of this person's working life. Assuming a starting age of 25, this means 40 years of constructive work for a minimum net savings of $320,000. Using this simple analogy, hiring only three disabled people will eventually save society one million dollars.[47]

Many librarians will be interested in the EEOC's observation that the "social benefits of decreasing support payments and increasing tax revenues by expanding the employment of the disabled seem particularly important currently as Federal, State and local governments are frequently confronting budget deficits."[48]

Concluding its review of the research regarding the economic impact of employment discrimination against people with disabilities, the EEOC declares that

> discrimination against disabled individuals can be viewed, like discrimination against minorities and women, as a market failure due to a taste for discrimination, short run profit maximizing, and/or use of imperfect information. It can also be viewed as an externality where others pay for the cost of an individual's disability, which becomes particularly problematic without government intervention because optimal investments in human capital (including accommodations) are not made. The effect of this failure is a reduction in national productivity that stems from use of a constricted labor market, failure to accurately return investments on human capital, failure to make optimal investments in human capital and/or use of imperfect information to predict productivity.[49]

In short, an entire society, including its infrastructure, culture, and government services and programs, suffers when inequities exist in the workplace; this is why discrimination against people with disabilities is now illegal in the United States. Our country simply cannot afford such a squandering of precious human and financial resources. To ensure that all employees are aware of their rights and responsibilities under the ADA, every "employer, employment agency, labor organization, or joint labor-management committee covered under this Title shall post notices in an accessible format to applicants, employees, and members describing the applicable provisions of this Act, in the manner prescribed by Section 711 of the Civil Rights Act of 1964."[50]

## PUBLIC SERVICES—TITLE II

Title II of the ADA simply states that "no qualified individual with a disability shall, by reason of such disability, be excluded from participation in or be denied the benefits of the services, programs, or activities of a public entity, or be subjected to discrimination by any such entity."[51] A "qualified individual with a disability" is defined as any person with a disability "who, with or without reasonable modifications to rules, policies, or practices, the removal of architectural, communication, or transportation barriers, or the provision of auxiliary aids and services, meets the essential eligibility requirements for the receipt of services or the participation in programs or activities provided by a public entity."[52]

All state and local governments, regardless of size, and "any department, agency, special purpose district, or other instrumentality of a State or States or local government" are included in the ADA definition of a "public entity."[53] Therefore, the vast majority of public libraries and their branches, as well as many academic and school libraries, must comply with the regulations for Title II by January 26, 1992.[54]

The Department of Justice regulations state that it is a violation of the ADA to "deny a qualified individual with a disability the opportunity to participate in or benefit from the aid, benefit, or service" of a public entity or to "afford a qualified individual with a disability an opportunity to participate in or benefit from the aid, benefit, or service that is not equal to that afforded others."[55] Furthermore, a public entity may not provide an individual with a disability with a "service that is not as effective in affording equal opportunity to obtain the same result" or furnish different services to individuals with disabilities than are provided to others "unless such action is necessary to provide qualified individuals with disabilities with aids, benefits, or services that are as effective as those provided to others."[56] Accordingly, every public entity must "administer services, programs, and activities in the most integrated setting appropriate to the needs of qualified individuals with disabilities."[57]

Essentially, the regulations to implement Title II are "intended to prohibit exclusion and segregation of individuals with disabilities and the denial of equal opportunities enjoyed by others, based on, among other things, presumptions, patronizing attitudes, fears, and stereotypes about individuals with disabilities."[58] As a result, public entities must "ensure that their actions are based on facts applicable to individuals and not on presumptions as to what a class of individuals with disabilities can or cannot do."[59]

The Department of Justice elaborates upon the antisegregation provisions of Title II by stating that

> Integration is fundamental to the purposes of the Americans with Disabilities Act. Provision of segregated accommodations and services relegates persons with disabilities to second-class status. For example, it would be a violation of this provision to require persons with disabilities to eat in the back room of a government cafeteria or to refuse to allow a person with a disability the full use of recreation or exercise facilities because of stereotypes about the person's ability to participate.[60]

Separate or different services for people with disabilities may be provided by a public entity "only when necessary to ensure that the aids, benefits, or services are as effective as those provided to others."[61] But even when separate programs would be permitted, people with disabilities cannot be prevented from participating in activities or programs that are not different or separate. The officials at the Department of Justice believe that

> This is an important and overearching principle of the Americans with Disabilities Act. Separate, special, or different programs that are designed to provide a benefit to persons with disabilities cannot be used to restrict the participation of persons with disabilities in general, integrated activities.[62]

A corollary of this rule is that nothing in the regulations for Title II "shall be construed to require an individual with a disability to accept an accommodation, aid, service, opportunity, or benefit provided under the ADA . . . which such individual chooses not to accept."[63] Basically, "modified participation for persons with disabilities must be a choice, not a requirement."[64]

It is also a violation of the ADA for a public entity to deny a qualified individual with a disability "the opportunity to participate as a member of planning or advisory boards."[65] Public entity libraries that provide financial aid or consultant services to other public libraries should note that Title II also prohibits the perpetuation of discrimination against people with disabilities "by providing significant assistance to an agency, organization, or person that discriminates on the basis of disability in providing any aid, benefit, or service to beneficiaries of the public entity's program."[66]

Title II requires that every public entity "take appropriate steps to ensure that communications with applicants, participants, and members of the public with disabilities are as effective as communications with others."[67] For a public entity to achieve effective communications, it must "furnish appropriate auxiliary aids and services where necessary to afford an individual with a disability an equal opportunity to participate in, and enjoy the benefits of a service, program, or activity conducted by a public entity" and, in deciding what type of auxiliary aid or service may be needed, the public entity must "give primary consideration to the requests of the individual with disabilities."[68]

The requirement to provide needed auxiliary aids and services will, perhaps more than any other ADA requirement, directly impact the operation of American libraries. Included in the list of required aids and services are:

(1) Qualified interpreters, notetakers, transcription services, written materials, telephone handset amplifiers, assistive listening systems, telephones compatible with hearing aids, closed caption decoders, open and closed captioning, telecommunications devices for deaf persons (TDDs), videotext displays, or other effective methods of making aurally delivered materials available to individuals with hearing impairments;

(2) Qualified readers, taped texts, audiorecordings, Brailled materials, large print materials, or other effective methods of making visually delivered materials available to individuals with visual impairments;

(3) Acquisition or modification of equipment or devices; and

(4) Other similar services and actions.[69]

Critical to understanding the public entity library's obligation to provide necessary auxiliary aids and services is the realization that this list "is not an all-inclusive or exhaustive catalogue of possible or available auxiliary aids or services. It is not possible to provide an exhaustive list, and an attempt to do so would omit the new devices that will become available with emerging technology."[70]

For example, after the Department of Justice released its proposed regulations for Title II, many commenters suggested that additional examples be added to the list of auxiliary aids and services, including

> . . . audio description services, secondary auditory programs, telebraillers, and reading machines. While the Department declines to add these items to the list, they are auxiliary aids and services and may be appropriate depending on the circumstances . . . . The Department, however, emphasizes that, although the definition would include 'state of the art' devices, public entities are not required to use the newest or most advanced technologies as long as the auxiliary aid or service that is selected affords effective communication.[71]

In addition, a public entity must allow "an opportunity for individuals with disabilities to request the auxiliary aids and services of their choice" and the "expressed choice shall be given primary consideration by the public entity."[72] The public entity is required to "honor the choice unless it can demonstrate that another effective means of communication exists or that use of the means chosen would not be required" under the regulations.[73] The Department of Justice clarifies this portion of the regulations by pointing out that

> Deference to the request of the individual with a disability is desirable because of the range of disabilities, the variety of auxiliary aids and services, and different circumstances requiring effective communication. For instance, some courtrooms are now equipped for 'computer-assisted transcripts,' which allow virtually instantaneous transcripts of courtroom argument and testimony to appear on displays. Such a system might be an effective auxiliary aid or service for a person who is deaf or has a hearing loss who uses speech to communicate, but may be useless for someone who uses sign language.
>
> Although in some circumstances a notepad and written materials may be sufficient to permit effective communication, in other circumstances they may not be sufficient. For example, a qualified interpreter may be necessary when information being communicated is complex, or is exchanged for a lengthy period of time. Generally, factors to be considered in determining whether an interpreter is required include the context in which the communication is taking place, the number of people involved, and the importance of the communication.[74]

This example can easily be extended to the library setting. While a notepad might provide effective communications for simple transactions at the circulation desk or basic directional inquiries, it clearly would not suffice for a puppet show or a complicated reference question. While it probably would be effective and feasible to read a brief excerpt from an almanac or an article from the *World Book Encyclopedia* to a person with a print disability, it would certainly be both impractical and ineffective for a librarian to read a complete article from the *Scientific American* or the full text of the *Kama Sutra of Vatsyayana* to a patron with a visual impairment. As a result, the Department of Justice has determined that

> Reading devices or readers should be provided when necessary for equal participation and opportunity to benefit from any governmental service, program, or activity, such as reviewing public documents, examining demonstrative evidence, and filling out voter registration forms or forms needed to receive public benefits . . . . Reading devices and readers are appropriate auxiliary aids and services where necessary to permit an individual with a disability to participate in or benefit from a service, program, or activity.[75]

Unless reading devices are available in public entity libraries, it will not be possible for people with limited vision to equally and independently benefit from a library collection of noncirculating reference materials. Magnification systems that enlarge the text of reading materials are also auxiliary aids and may be helpful to some library users.

Libraries must make large print, taped, and Braille reading materials available for loan to any qualified individual with visual disabilities who needs them. Since these formats of reading materials are explicitly included in the Department of Justice's list of auxiliary aids and services, there can be little doubt that each public entity library must provide them in appropriate quantities if requested by any reader with a print disability who is otherwise qualified to receive services from the library. While private entity libraries are not required to actually stock accessible or special goods, such as Braille books, they must interlibrary loan these materials if desired by an eligible user; no such loophole in the requirement to provide these needed auxiliary aids and services exists in the regulations covering public entity libraries.[76]

The only limitation to a public entity's obligation to provide appropriate auxiliary aids and services occurs when the entity can demonstrate that the provision of the needed aid or service "would result in a fundamental alteration in the nature of a service, program, or activity or in undue financial and administrative burdens."[77] In those cases where the personnel of a public entity may believe that the provision of a proposed auxiliary aid or service would result in such alterations or burdens, the decision must be made by the head of the public entity or his or her designee after considering all resources available for use in the funding and operation of the service, program, or activity and must be accompanied by a written statement of the reasons for reaching that conclusion. If an action required to comply with this subpart would result in such an alteration or such burdens, a public entity shall take any other action that would not result in such an alteration or such burdens but would nevertheless ensure that, to the maximum extent possible, individuals with disabilities receive the benefits or services provided by the public entity.[78]

In taking any action required by Title II, librarians will be happy to know (as professionals that have opposed supplemental service fees in the past) that a public entity is prohibited from placing "a surcharge on a particular individual with a disability or any group of individuals with disabilities to cover the cost of measures, such as the provision of auxiliary aids or program accessibility, that are required to provide that individual or group with the nondiscriminatory treatment required by the Act or this part."[79] This would prohibit such actions as charging a person who uses sign language for the cost of interpreter services or requiring that an individual who is homebound because of a disability pay for the postage costs of books-by-mail service.

The regulations for Title II take a slightly different approach for one special auxiliary aid—the Telecommunications Device for Deaf persons (TDD), also referred to as a text telephone. The regulations clearly state that "where a public entity communicates by telephone with applicants and beneficiaries, TDDs or equally effective telecommunications systems shall be used to communicate with individuals with impaired hearing or speech."[80] But Title IV of the ADA amends the Communications Act of 1934 to require that common carriers establish telecommunications relay services, which allow a person using a text telephone to call a hearing person (or vice versa) through an operator, no later than July 26, 1993.[81] Although the regulations for Title II state that "where relay services, such as those required by Title IV of the ADA are available, a public entity may use those services to meet the requirements" for effective communications,[82] the deadline for the establishment of telecommunications relay services falls 18 months after public entities must comply with the requirements of Title II. Therefore, many public libraries may not have the option of relying on relay services and will therefore need to acquire and install a text telephone during 1992.

The question also arises as to whether future telecommunications relay services will be effective for all types of telephone transactions, such as complex reference inquiries. The Department of Justice therefore

> encourages those entities that have extensive telephone contact with the public such as city halls, public libraries, and public aid offices, to have TDDs to insure more immediate access. When the provision of telephone service is a major function of the entity, TDDs should be available.[83]

Yet another problem surrounding the public library choice between using an in-house text telephone or the relay services involves the ethics of patron confidentiality. While Title IV of the ADA prohibits relay operators from refusing or limiting calls or from "disclosing the content of any relayed conversation and from keeping records of the content of any such conversation beyond the duration of the call,"[84] the library profession may not be willing to compromise the confidentiality of library services by utilizing relay systems. The Department of Justice acknowledges that

> the communication through relay systems may not be appropriate in cases of crimelines pertaining to rape, domestic violence, child abuse, and drugs. The Department believes that it is more appropriate for the Federal Communications Commission to address these issues in its rulemaking under Title IV.[85]

It will be the responsibility of the library profession to examine its own code of confidentiality in order to determine how, or if, the possible use of nondirect telecommunications with patrons who have hearing or speech impairments fits into the issues of library service ethics.

The regulations to implement Title II also address physical accessibility to public entity facilities by stating that "no qualified individual with a disability shall, because a public entity's facilities are inaccessible to or unusable by individuals with disabilities, be excluded from participation in, or be denied the benefits of the services . . . of a public entity."[86] Every public entity must operate each service and program so that "when viewed in its entirety, [it] is readily accessible to and usable by individuals with disabilities."[87]

This requirement does not necessarily mean that every public entity must make all of its existing facilities accessible to people with disabilities, nor must any action be taken "that would destroy the historic significance of an historic property."[88] Neither must a public entity "take any action that it can demonstrate would result in a fundamental alteration in the nature of a service, program, or activity or in undue financial and administrative burdens."[89] In those instances where the personnel of a public entity believe that the removal of architectural barriers would fundamentally alter the service provided or would constitute an undue burden, the entity must follow the same procedures as in the case of a request for an auxiliary aid or service. Even when a requested action can be proven by a public entity to constitute an undue burden or fundamental alteration in the nature of the service, the public entity must "take any other action that would not result in such alteration or such burdens but would nevertheless ensure that individuals with disabilities receive the benefits or services provided by the public entity."[90]

This point can be illustrated by considering a public library located in an historic building accessible only by spiral staircase. Assuming that the library administration can prove that removal or ramping of the staircase would involve undue financial burdens or would destroy the historic significance of the facility, the library would still have to provide any other modified services or auxiliary aids that do not constitute such burdens. For example, videocassettes with closed captioning would need to be included in the library's circulating collection (if the library has videos) and books in formats accessible to people with visual impairments would be needed, since the spiral staircase would not necessarily prevent individuals with hearing or visual disabilities from utilizing the library. For individuals with mobility impairments, the library would need to provide alternative service delivery, such as curbside service.

It is the opinion of the Department of Justice that compliance with the public entity requirement to remove architectural barriers "would in most cases not result in undue financial and administrative burdens on a public entity. In determining whether financial and administrative burdens are undue, all public entity resources available for use in the funding and operation of the service, program, or activity should be considered."[91]

A public entity may comply with the requirement to provide physically accessible services and programs through such means as the

> redesign of equipment, reassignment of services to accessible build-
> ings, assignment of aides to beneficiaries, home visits, delivery of
> services at alternate accessible sites, alteration of existing facilities and
> construction of new facilities, use of accessible rolling stock or other
> conveyances, or any other methods that result in making its services,
> programs, or activities readily accessible to and usable by individuals

with disabilities. A public entity is not required to make structural changes in existing facilities where other methods are effective in achieving compliance . . . . In choosing among available methods for meeting the requirements . . . a public entity shall give priority to those methods that offer services, programs, and activities to qualified individuals with disabilities in the most integrated setting appropriate.[92]

In the event that structural changes to existing facilities are undertaken by a public entity as a result of the ADA, "such changes shall be made within three years of January 26, 1992, but in any event as expeditiously as possible."[93]

In addition, every public entity that employs 50 or more workers "shall develop, within six months of January 26, 1992, a transition plan setting forth the steps necessary to complete such changes" and must "provide an opportunity to interested persons, including individuals with disabilities or organizations representing individuals with disabilities, to participate in the development of the transition plan by submitting comments."[94]

The transition plan must, at a minimum:

(i) Identify physical obstacles in the public entity's facilities that limit the accessibility of its programs or activities to individuals with disabilities;

(ii) Describe in detail the methods that will be used to make the facilities accessible,

(iii) Specify the schedule for taking the steps necessary to achieve compliance . . . and, if the time period of the transition plan is longer than one year, identify steps that will be taken during each year of the transition period; and

(iv) Indicate the official responsible for implementation of the plan.[95]

A copy of the completed transition plan must be made available for public inspection and, although not specifically stated in the regulations, be produced in accessible formats.

The regulations for Title II also stipulate that each newly constructed or altered facility used by a public entity be "readily accessible to and usable by individuals with disabilities" if construction or alteration started after January 26, 1992.[96] Public entities may choose to comply with either the Uniform Federal Accessibility Standards (UFAS)[97] or the new Americans with Disabilities Act Accessibility Guidelines for Buildings and Facilities (ADAAG),[98] "except that, if ADAAG is chosen, the elevator exemption . . . does not apply."[99] The "elevator exemption" refers to the fact that, with some nonlibrary exceptions, ADAAG does not require the installation of elevators "in facilities that are less than three stories or have less than 3000 square feet per story" while UFAS permits "no such exemption."[100] Since Section 501(a) of the ADA makes it clear that "nothing in this Act shall be construed to apply a lesser standard than the standards applied under Title V of the Rehabilitation Act of 1973 (29 U.S.C. 790 et seq.) or the regulations issued by Federal agencies pursuant to such title,"[101] and since UFAS represents the standards used to implement Section 504 of the Rehabilitation Act of 1973, public entities who choose to follow ADAAG are not entitled to the elevator exemption.[102] Thus, a two-story public library built after January 1992 must have an elevator, whether designed to meet the specifications of UFAS or ADAAG.

The architectural requirements of ADAAG are extensive and complex, consuming more than 130 pages and including some six dozen technical tables and diagrams. Specifications are provided for space allowance and reach ranges, accessible routes, protruding objects, floors, parking spaces, curbs, ramps, stairs, elevators, platform lifts, windows, doors, restrooms, water fountains, signage, alarms, telephones, meeting rooms, and other features of buildings. Additional requirements apply only to libraries, and cover reading and study areas, check-out desks, card catalogs, magazine displays, and stacks.[103] For example, card catalogs and magazine displays may not exceed a height of 54 inches, with a maximum height of 48 inches preferred.[104]

It is interesting to note that some who commented on the proposed version of ADAAG asked for the Architectural and Transportation Barriers Compliance Board to consider and clarify the requirements for online public access catalogs, in light of their predominance in libraries and the inability of those with substantial visual impairments to use traditional card catalogs.[105] The Board responded to this inquiry in the final version of ADAAG by stating that the "issue of Braille/voice input/output terminals is an operational matter and is under the purview of the Department of Justice and is not addressed in these guidelines."[106] In other words, the library catalog is both a fixed furnishing covered by the specifications of ADAAG and a service that must be in compliance with the requirements of Title II.

In order to facilitate effective compliance with the regulations for Title II of the ADA, every public entity, irrespective of size or budget, must "evaluate its current services, policies, and practices, and the effects thereof, that do not or may not meet the requirements . . . and, to the extent modification . . . is required . . . proceed to make the necessary modifications."[107] Of course, each public entity must "provide an opportunity to interested persons, including individuals with disabilities or organizations representing individuals with disabilities, to participate in the self-evaluation process by submitting comments."[108] Public entities that employ 50 or more workers must, "for at least three years following completion of the self-evaluation, maintain on file and make available for public inspection a list of the interested persons consulted, a description of areas examined and any problems identified, and . . . any modifications made."[109]

According to the Department of Justice, experience "has demonstrated the self-evaluation process to be a valuable means of establishing a working relationship with individuals with disabilities."[110] The creation of such relationships is essential to ADA compliance, since the removal of an architectural barrier today does not mean that a new obstacle will not be erected tomorrow. Likewise, a library might acquire accessible reading materials in 1992 and then discard them in 1995, or begin a program of service to homebound individuals with a disability and subsequently discontinue the service after budget sequestrations or the expiration of grant funding. The ongoing input of people with disabilities will help to ensure that these unfortunate events do not occur.

Consumer involvement is also critical to the process of ADA compliance because the needs of individuals with disabilities cannot possibly be guessed or inferred; only by asking current and potential library users with disabilities what modifications are needed can libraries hope to achieve equitable services. The importance of this principle has been recognized in the literature on rehabilitation:

> We have a system in which the programs are designed by the very people who will benefit from them in terms of professional power, prestige, and income. Unfortunately, the input of people with disabilities is solicited only occasionally, and even though many centers have consumer advisory panels, these groups have no authority to shape programs or allocate resources. **Disabled people have little say in what services will be offered by a rehabilitation center, since very few centers have even asked clients what they need and want.** We professionals determine what disabled people need. Consumers have little say as to what will be the content of research into the nature or course of their disabilities. We professionals who are not experiencing those disabilities determine what needs to be studied. Now, no one would propose that disabled people without professional or scientific training are fully qualified to define the total program of research nationally. Yet, we professionals with scientific training but without the experience of living with the disability feel fully qualified to plan such

programs. Isn't this a double standard? . . . We all go to professional conferences and participate in our annual self-congratulation sessions in which we reassure ourselves that we are advancing the state of the art. But who defines the state of the art? Thus, we professionals often operate within a realm that greatly differs from the reality that is lived by [a] person with disabilities, and because of our **social** isolation from people with disabilities, we seldom realize how wide the schism is.[111]

Current and prospective library users with disabilities understand how broad the gulf is between their needs and the services and materials usually provided by libraries; rehabilitationists and even the attorneys at the Department of Justice apparently comprehend it. Is it possible that public librarians, whose basic mission involves the provision of services to all, do not?

In conjunction with the required self-evaluation process, each public entity must "disseminate sufficient information to applicants, participants, beneficiaries, and other interested persons to inform them of their rights and protections afforded by the ADA" and the regulations.[112] The Department of Justice indicates that

Methods of providing this information include, for example, the publication of information in handbooks, manuals, and pamphlets that are distributed to the public to describe a public entity's programs and activities; the display of informative posters in service centers and other public places; or the broadcast of information by television or radio.[113]

Obviously, this information will need to be provided in formats usable by people with disabilities. Libraries, as the chief information providers for many public entities, clearly have a major role to play in the public education processes mandated by the ADA.

In addition to the foregoing requirements, every "public entity that employs 50 or more persons shall designate at least one employee to coordinate its efforts to comply" with Title II, "including any investigation of any complaint communicated to it alleging its noncompliance . . . or alleging any actions that would be prohibited" by the regulations for Title II.[114] The Department of Justice defends the need for an ADA coordinator by explaining that

The requirements for designation of a particular employee and dissemination of information about how to locate that employee helps to ensure that individuals dealing with large agencies are able to easily find a responsible person who is familiar with the requirements of the Act . . . and communicate those requirements to other individuals in the agency who may be unaware of their responsibilities. This . . . in no way limits a public entity's obligation to ensure that all of its employees comply with the requirements . . . but it ensures that any failure by individual employees can be promptly corrected by the designated employee.[115]

Each public entity must also establish a grievance procedure for resolving complaints of violations under the regulations for Title II. It is the view of the Department of Justice that public entities

> should be required to establish a mechanism for resolution of complaints at the local level without requiring the complainant to resort to the federal complaint procedures . . . Complainants would not, however, be required to exhaust the public entity's grievance procedures before filling a complaint [under the federal regulations].[116]

If a complaint from a library user with a disability is filed under the federal procedures, the Department of Education shall have the responsibility of reviewing the complaint,[117] but the aggrieved individual may also direct the complaint to "any agency that provides funding to the public entity that is the subject of the complaint, or with the Department of Justice for referral" to the appropriate agency.[118] The designated reviewing agency will investigate the complaint and seek to obtain voluntary compliance on the part of the public entity if a violation of the ADA has occurred. In the event that an aggrieved individual with a disability must seek judicial relief, the court may allow the prevailing party a reasonable attorney's fee, including litigation expenses and costs.[119]

Of course, for a public entity library, the price of such legal action would be much higher than mere court costs or attorney fees; the library's entire public relations efforts to date could be undone by only one legitimate complaint filed by a reader with a disability. For this reason, all public entity librarians should be familiar with the ADA and its regulations and should implement changes in programs, services, materials, and equipment as soon as possible.

## PUBLIC ACCOMMODATIONS AND SERVICES PROVIDED BY PRIVATE ENTITIES—TITLE III

Title III of the ADA prohibits discrimination on the basis of disability in the provision of services provided by nonpublic entities, including any "museum, library, gallery, or other place of public display or collection."[120] The Act requires that these entities allow each person with a disability "the full and equal enjoyment of the goods, services, facilities, privileges, advantages, or accommodations of any place of public accommodation"[121] and stipulates that services must "be afforded to an individual with a disability in the most integrated setting appropriate to the needs of the individual."[122] It is important for librarians to understand that nearly every American library not covered by Title II (Public Services) must comply with the nondiscriminatory requirements of Title III by January 26, 1992.

The regulations designed to implement Title III, issued by the Department of Justice, explain that "full and equal enjoyment" of services means that every individual with a disability who is otherwise eligible to receive the services of a privately funded library has the right to participate in the library's programs and services and must be provided "an equal opportunity to obtain the same results as others to the extent possible with such accommodations as may be required" by the ADA.[123] In determining eligibility for the receipt of services provided by a private entity, the public accommodation may not apply or impose "criteria that screen out or tend to screen out an individual with a disability" unless the criteria "can be shown to be necessary for the provision of the goods, services, facilities, privileges, advantages, or accommodations being offered."[124] In addition, a library covered by the regulations for Title III of the ADA "may not impose a surcharge on a particular individual with a disability or any group of individuals with disabilities to cover the costs of measures" required for compliance.[125]

As with public entity libraries, those libraries covered by the regulations for Title III must make reasonable modifications in policies, practices, or procedures when necessary to provide services for people with disabilities, "unless the public accommodation can demonstrate that making the modifications would fundamentally alter the nature of the goods, services, facilities, privileges, advantages, or accommodations."[126] Accordingly, Title III libraries must offer auxiliary aids and services if needed by an eligible reader to benefit from the library's services, unless the provision of the needed aids or services would require "significant difficulty or expense."[127]

The requirement to provide needed auxiliary aids and services in private libraries is similar to the obligation of public entity libraries discussed earlier. The Department of Justice clarifies this responsibility by pointing out that implicit in the duty to make needed auxiliary aids and services available "is the underlying obligation of a public accommodation to communicate effectively with its customers, clients, patients, or participants who have disabilities affecting hearing, vision, or speech."[128] Of course, there is some flexibility in the requirement to offer auxiliary aids and services:

> A public accommodation can choose among various alternatives as long as the result is effective communication. For example, a restaurant would not be required to provide menus in Braille for patrons who are blind, if the waiters in the restaurant are made available to read the menu. Similarly, a clothing boutique would not be required to have Brailled price tags if sales personnel provide price information orally upon request; and a bookstore would not be required to make available a sign language interpreter, because effective communication can be conducted by notepad.[129]

As stated previously in the discussion of Title II's regulations, this requirement presents unique problems in the library environment. For example, it would be relatively easy for the staff of a library subject to the requirements of Title III to read a brochure to a patron with a print disability, but a request for the librarian to read the complete text of an issue of the *Journal of the American Medical Association* could probably not be reasonably handled without the presence of a reading machine. While a simple directional inquiry could be answered by using a notepad with a reader with a hearing impairment, this means of communication would be difficult to use during a complicated reference transaction. The Department of Justice does not find it

> difficult to imagine a wide range of communications involving areas such as health, legal matters, and finances that would be sufficiently lengthy or complex to require an interpreter for effective communication. In some situations, an effective alternative to use of a notepad or an interpreter may be the use of a computer terminal upon which the representative of the public accommodation and the customer or client can exchange typewritten messages.[130]

There is, however, a difference in the requirement for the provision of special format library materials for entities covered by Title III. Known as "accessible or special goods," these special format items include "Brailled versions of books, books on audio cassettes, closed-captioned videotapes" and other specialized materials.[131] A library operated by a private entity is not required "to alter its inventory to include accessible or special goods that are designed for, or facilitate use by, individuals with disabilities," but must interlibrary loan these materials "at the request of an individual with disabilities, if, in the normal course of its operation, it makes special orders on unstocked goods, and if the accessible or special goods can be obtained from a supplier with whom the public accommodation customarily does business."[132] As a result, public entity libraries must actually stock appropriate collections of special format materials if needed by eligible users with disabilities, while Title III libraries must only interlibrary loan these materials when requested.

Since many libraries also present audiovisual programs in addition to or instead of providing these materials for circulation to borrowers, it is important to note that movie theaters are not required to show open-captioned films but "other public accommodations that impart verbal information through soundtracks on films, videotapes, or slide shows are required to make such information accessible to persons with hearing impairments."[133] This might be achieved through using a sign language interpreter or presenting open-captioned audiovisual materials, depending on the circumstances and the need of the individual with the disability. Likewise, "tape players used for an audioguided tour of a museum exhibit may require the addition of Brailled adhesive labels to the buttons on a reasonable number of the tape players to facilitate their use by individuals who are blind."[134] This need for Braille labels can be extended to library photocopiers, online public access catalogs, computers, and other equipment available for patron use.

The requirements for Title II libraries to acquire text telephones or TDDs, as previously discussed, also apply to libraries covered by the regulations of Title III; private entity librarians will also need to carefully weigh the questions surrounding the choice between the use of telephone relay services or text telephones. The regulations for the implementation of Title III also stipulate that "a public accommodation that offers a customer . . . the opportunity to make outgoing telephone calls on more than an incidental convenience basis shall make available, upon request, a TDD for the use of an individual who has impaired hearing or a communication disorder."[135]

Of course, as with public entity libraries, in the event that a requested auxiliary aid or service would result in an undue burden or would fundamentally alter the nature of the service provided, the public accommodation must still offer "an alternative auxiliary aid or service, if one exists, that would not result in an alteration or such burden but would nevertheless ensure that, to the maximum extent possible, individuals with disabilities receive the . . . services . . . offered by the public accommodation."[136]

Libraries covered by Title III of the ADA must also "remove architectural barriers in existing facilities, including communication barriers that are structural in nature, where such removal is readily achievable, i.e., easily accomplishable and able to be carried out without much difficulty or expense."[137] According to the Department of Justice, examples of removing barriers in existing facilities include but are not limited to:

(1) Installing ramps;

(2) Making curb cuts in sidewalks and entrances;

(3) Repositioning shelves;

(4) Rearranging tables, chairs, vending machines, display racks, and other furniture;

(5) Repositioning telephones;

(6) Adding raised markings on elevator control buttons;

(7) Installing flashing alarm lights;

(8) Widening doors;

(9) Installing offset hinges to widen doorways;

(10) Eliminating a turnstile or providing an alternative accessible path;

(11) Installing accessible door hardware;

(12) Installing grab bars in toilet stalls;

(13) Rearranging toilet partitions to increase maneuvering space;

(14) Insulating lavatory pipes under sinks to prevent burns;

(15) Installing a raised toilet seat;

(16) Installing a full-length bathroom mirror;

(17) Repositioning the paper towel dispenser in a bathroom;

(18) Creating designated accessible parking spaces;

(19) Installing an accessible paper cup dispenser at an existing inaccessible water fountain;

(20) Removing high pile, low density carpeting; or

(21) Installing vehicle hand controls.[138]

This list of examples is not exhaustive but reflects "modest measures that may be taken to remove barriers and that are likely to be readily achievable."[139] As the Department of Justice points out:

> The readily achievable defense requires a less demanding level of exertion by a public accommodation than does the undue burden defense to the auxiliary aids requirements . . . . In that sense, it can be characterized as a "lower" standard than the undue burden standard. The readily achievable defense is also less demanding than the undue

hardship defense in Section 102(b)(5) of the ADA, which limits the obligation to make reasonable accommodation in employment. Barrier removal measures that are not easily accomplishable and are not able to be carried out without much difficulty or expense are not required under the readily achievable standard, even if they do not impose an undue burden or undue hardship.[140]

The responsibility to remove barriers when readily achievable is a continuing one since, as time passes, removal that originally "was not readily achievable may later be required because of changed circumstances."[141] For this reason, the Department of Justice

> urges public accommodations to establish procedures for an ongoing assessment of their compliance with the ADA's barrier removal requirements. The Department recommends that this process include appropriate consultation with individuals with disabilities or organizations representing them. A serious effort at self-assessment can diminish the threat of litigation and save resources by identifying the most efficient means of providing required access.[142]

When a public accommodation provided by a private entity "can demonstrate that barrier removal is not readily achievable, the public accommodation shall not fail to make its goods, services, facilities, privileges, advantages, or accommodations available through alternative methods, if those methods are readily achievable."[143] For example, it might not be readily achievable to lower, remove, or raise shelving or to rearrange display racks in a retail store, but

> the store must, if readily achievable, provide a clerk or take other alternative methods to retrieve inaccessible merchandise. Similarly, if it is not readily achievable to ramp a long flight of stairs leading to the front door of a restaurant or pharmacy, the restaurant or pharmacy must take alternative measures, if readily achievable, such as providing curb service or home delivery.[144]

The ADA and its regulations for Title III entities also make it a violation to fail "to design and construct facilities for first occupancy later than 30 months after the date of enactment (i.e., after January 26, 1993) that are readily accessible to and usable by individuals with disabilities."[145] According to the Department of Justice, the requirement to provide accessibility

> contemplates a high degree of convenient access. It is intended to ensure that patrons and employees of places of public accommodation and employees of commercial facilities are able to get to, enter, and use the facility.[146]

It is important to remember that the ADA is

> geared to the future—its goal being that, over time, access will be the rule, rather than the exception. Thus, the Act only requires modest expenditures . . . to provide access to existing facilities not otherwise being altered, but requires all new construction and alterations to be accessible.[147]

As with their public entity counterparts, libraries subject to the requirements of Title III must comply with the requirements of the ADA Accessibility Guidelines for Buildings and Facilities (ADAAG),[148] which were discussed earlier, unless to do so would be "structurally impracticable."[149] This would occur "only in those rare instances when the unique characteristics of terrain prevent the incorporation of accessibility features."[150] For example, a library operated by a private entity that "must be built on stilts because of its location in marshlands or over water"[151] need not be accessible to individuals who use wheelchairs if it is structurally impracticable to do so; of course, such a bizarre library would still need to provide print magnification systems, reading devices, closed-caption decoders, and be otherwise "made accessible for individuals with vision or hearing impairments or other kinds of disabilities,"[152] unless an undue burden would result.

Any person with a disability who believes that discrimination on the basis of disability has occurred or "who has reasonable grounds for believing that such person is about to be subjected to discrimination . . . may institute a civil action for preventative relief, including an application for a permanent or temporary injunction, restraining order, or other order."[153] In addition, "the court may, in its discretion, permit the Attorney General to intervene in the civil action if the Attorney General or his or her designee certifies that the case is of general importance" or, at any time, "the Attorney General may commence a civil action in any appropriate United States district court if the Attorney General has reasonable cause to believe" that a violation has occurred or is about to occur.[154]

No civil actions may be brought, however, against private entities that employ 25 or fewer workers and have gross receipts of $1 million a year or less until July 26, 1992, or against those with 10 or less employees or gross receipts under $500,001 before July 26, 1993.[155] When civil actions occur as a result of a public accommodation's failure to comply with Title III, the court may grant temporary, preliminary, or permanent relief, including requiring the provision of an auxiliary aid or service or the removal of architectural barriers.[156] In addition, the court may award any other "relief as the court considers appropriate, including monetary damages to persons aggrieved when requested by the Attorney General," but may not impose punitive damages.[157] However, "to vindicate the public interest," the court may "assess a civil penalty" not to exceed $50,000 for a first violation and $100,000 for any subsequent violations.[158]

While the requirements of the ADA and its regulations certainly represent a major challenge to all libraries, they also provide a unique opportunity for librarians to reach previously unserved or underserved clientele. By seeking the input of readers with disabilities and performing evaluations and reviews of existing programs, activities, and services, librarians in both public and private libraries can ensure that the freedom to read is a reality for all library users and not merely a slogan paraded on banners during National Library Week. Only by working together to achieve equality in service can people with disabilities and librarians guarantee that libraries will remain "temples of happiness and wisdom common to us all."[159]

## REFERENCES

1. Americans with Disabilities Act (ADA) of 1990, Section 2(6)(1).

2. American Civil Liberties Union, AIDS Project, ADA Education Project, *The Americans with Disabilities Act: What It Means for People Living with AIDS* (New York: ACLU Foundation, 1991),unpaged.

3. Richard Thornburgh, "A Note from the Attorney General," introduction to *The Americans with Disabilities Act: Questions and Answers* (Washington, DC: Department of Justice, 1991).

4. ADA, Section 2(a)(1).

5. ADA, Section 3(2).

6. 56 *Federal Register* 35735.

7. 56 *Federal Register* 35741.

8. Lewis E. Kraus and Susan Stoddard,*Chartbook on Disability in the United States* (Washington, DC: National Institute on Disability and Rehabilitation Research, 1989), 3.

9. Ibid., 6-7.

10. U.S. Department of Education, Office of Special Education and Rehabilitative Services, *To Assure the Free Appropriate Public Education of All Children with Disabilities: Thirteenth Annual Report to Congress on the Implementation of the Individuals with Disabilities Education Act* (Washington, DC: U.S. Department of Education, 1991), 16-17.

11. Kraus and Stoddard, *Chartbook*, 21.

12. ADA, Section 2(a)(2).

13. ADA, Section 2(a)(7).

14. ADA, Section 2(a)(5).

15. ADA, Section 2(a)(8).

16. ADA, Section 2(a)(9).

17. ADA, Section 2(b)(2).

18. ADA, Section 2(b)(3).

19. ADA, Section 2(b)(4).

20. ADA, Section 102(a).

21. 56 *Federal Register* 35735.

22. ADA, Sections 101(5)(A) and 108.

23. ADA, Section 101(5)(B). The Rehabilitation Act of 1973 prohibited entities receiving federal financial assistance from discriminating against people with disabilities.

24. 56 *Federal Register* 35719.

25. ADA, Section 509(c)(4).

26. ADA, Section 103(c)(2).

27. 56 *Federal Register* 35752.

28. 56 *Federal Register* 35735.

29. 56 *Federal Register* 35727.

30. 56 *Federal Register* 35736.

31. Ibid.

32. ADA, Section 102(b)(1).

33. ADA, Section 102(b)(5)(A).

34. ADA, Section 102(b)(5)(B).

35. ADA, Section 101(9)(A).

36. ADA, Section 101(9)(B).

37. 56 *Federal Register* 35747.

38. 56 *Federal Register* 35736.

39. 56 *Federal Register* 35726.

40. ADA, Section 101(10)(A).

41. ADA, Section 101(10)(B).

42. 56 *Federal Register* 35745.

43. Ibid.

44. ADA, Section 102(c)(2).

45. ADA, Section 102(c)(3).

46. 56 *Federal Register* 8585.

47. Bonnie P. Tucker, "Section 504 of the Rehabilitation Act After Ten Years of Enforcement: The Past and the Future," *University of Illinois Law Review*, 1989, no. 4:890.

48. 56 *Federal Register* 8585.

49. 56 *Federal Register* 8582.

50. ADA, Section 105.

51. ADA, Section 202.

52. ADA, Section 201(2).

53. ADA, Section 201(1).

54. ADA, Section 205(a).

55. 56 *Federal Register*, 35718.

56. Ibid.

57. 56 *Federal Register* 35719.

58. 56 *Federal Register* 35703.

59. Ibid.

60. Ibid.

61. Ibid.

62. Ibid.

63. 56 *Federal Register* 35719.

64. 56 *Federal Register* 35703.

65. 56 *Federal Register* 35718.

66. Ibid.

67. 56 *Federal Register* 35721.

68. Ibid.

69. 56 *Federal Register* 35717.

70. 56 *Federal Register* 35697.

71. Ibid.

72. 56 *Federal Register* 35711.

73. 56 *Federal Register* 35711-35712.

74. 56 *Federal Register* 35712.

75. Ibid.

76. See 56 *Federal Register* 35598.

77. 56 *Federal Register* 35721.

78. Ibid.

79. 56 *Federal Register* 35719.

80. 56 *Federal Register* 35721.

81. ADA, Section 401.

82. 56 *Federal Register* 35712.

83. Ibid.

84. ADA, Section 401(d)(F).

85. 56 *Federal Register* 35712. Note, however, that the FCC chose not to address these issues directly in its final rules for Title IV. (See 56 *Federal Register* 36729-36733.)

86. 56 *Federal Register* 35719.

87. 56 *Federal Register* 35719-35720.

88. 56 *Federal Register* 35720.

89. Ibid.

90. Ibid.

91. 56 *Federal Register* 35709.

92. 56 *Federal Register* 35720.

93. Ibid.

94. Ibid.

95. Ibid.

96. Ibid.

97. U.S. General Services Administration et al., *Uniform Federal Accessibility Standards* (Washington, DC: GPO, 1988).

98. 56 *Federal Register* 35408-35542.

99. 56 *Federal Register* 35710.

100. Ibid.

101. ADA, Section 501(a).

102. 56 *Federal Register* 35720.

103. 56 *Federal Register* 35520.

104. 56 *Federal Register* 35520-35521.

105. Michael G. Gunde and Ruth O'Donnell. Letter to Architectural and Transportation Barriers Compliance Board, 4 March 1991.

106. 56 *Federal Register* 35447.

107. 56 *Federal Register* 35718.

108. Ibid.

109. Ibid.

110. 56 *Federal Register* 35701.

111. Roberta B. Trieschmann, *Aging with a Disability* (New York: Demos Publications, 1987), 54.

112. 56 *Federal Register* 35702.

113. Ibid.

114. 56 *Federal Register* 35718.

115. 56 *Federal Register* 35702.

116. 56 *Federal Register* 35713.

117. 56 *Federal Register* 35722.

118. 56 *Federal Register* 35721.

119. 56 *Federal Register* 35722.

120. ADA, Section 301(7)(H).

121. ADA, Section 302(a).

122. ADA, Section 302(b)(1)(B).
123. 56 *Federal Register* 35555.
124. 56 *Federal Register* 35596.
125. Ibid.
126. Ibid.
127. 56 *Federal Register* 35597.
128. 56 *Federal Register* 35565.
129. 56 *Federal Register* 35566.
130. 56 *Federal Register* 35567.
131. 56 *Federal Register* 35598.
132. Ibid.
133. 56 *Federal Register* 35567.
134. Ibid.
135. 56 *Federal Register* 35597.
136. Ibid.
137. Ibid.
138. Ibid.
139. 56 *Federal Register* 35568.
140. 56 *Federal Register* 35569.
141. Ibid.
142. Ibid.
143. 56 *Federal Register* 35598.
144. 56 *Federal Register* 35570.
145. 56 *Federal Register* 35574.
146. Ibid.
147. Ibid.
148. 56 *Federal Register* 35602.
149. 56 *Federal Register* 35600.
150. Ibid.
151. 56 *Federal Register* 35577.
152. 56 *Federal Register* 35578.
153. 56 *Federal Register* 35602.
154. Ibid.
155. 56 *Federal Register* 35603.
156. Ibid.
157. Ibid.
158. Ibid.
159. John Cotton Dana, "Meaning of the Public Library in a City's Life," *Library Journal* (1902): 755.

# CHAPTER 2
# Planning to Implement the ADA in the Library

## RUTH O'DONNELL

## INTRODUCTION

The Americans with Disabilities Act (ADA) allows citizens with disabilities to fully participate in opportunities made available by publicly supported and privately provided entities. Libraries provide some of the many publicly available opportunities that citizens are interested in accessing: opportunities to find the information they need, to enjoy their leisure time, and to develop their intellectual and vocational potential. Library managers must concern themselves with this law and its requirements.

This chapter on implementing the ADA in the library provides some suggestions, information, and resources for library managers who are ready to learn about the law and what it means for their organization. It is not a cookbook, nor is it a prescription that organizations can follow and expect to be in compliance when they have carried out the proposed action steps. Compliance with the ADA is dependent on whether or not an entity eliminates discrimination against individuals with disabilities. The law and the related federal regulations recognize various methods of doing that, and rely on the entity to develop approaches that will meet the needs of the individuals who want to participate in the opportunities provided by that entity. The service user then has recourse to appeals if he or she feels discriminated against.

The intent of the ADA to eliminate discrimination suggests a comprehensive approach to planning for implementation; libraries must look at all their facilities, programs, and services. A six-step model is presented for planning that can be used in any library setting, regardless of type or population served. The ADA discusses library services available to the public in two separate titles, Title II (Public Services) and Title III (Public Accommodations and Services Operated by Private Entities). The regulations for these two types of service are also separate. The language and requirements of the Public Services regulation are referred to in this chapter, since so many libraries are operated by public entities. Managers of privately operated libraries are encouraged to apply the planning method suggested here to their libraries and to use the Title III regulations for clarification.

Title I (Employment) of the ADA applies to all public entity employers, effective January 26, 1992, and to all private employers who employ 25 or more people, effective July 26, 1992, and 15 or more people, effective July 26, 1994. Some strategies for preparing to meet the ADA requirements for employment are also provided in this chapter.

The planning model described here has a beginning, but no end, since it recommends a continuous cycle of activity to ensure access to library services and programs for individuals with disabilities.

## SIX-STEP ADA PLANNING MODEL

Gathering information about the Americans with Disability Act and your library is Step One. The assignment of this responsibility to a library representative—the ADA coordinator—is Step Two. A self-evaluation study is Step Three. In Step Four, a planning approach is described. Step Five puts the plan into action and Step Six is an ongoing review of the continuing accessible service. The further description of each of these six steps includes a justification of why the step is necessary and suggested methods of carrying out the step. Further resources that can be consulted are provided in the following five lists at the end of this chapter:

Americans with Disabilities Act—Resources

Library Service for People with Disabilities—Resources

Organizations for People with Disabilities

Auxiliary Aids

Employment—Resources

The information provided here on implementing service strategies, Step Five, is quite brief. Were it to include all the information needed, it would be several volumes long. Fortunately, a great deal of how-to information on library service for people with disabilities has been published and is readily available. (See the second list of resources at the end of this chapter, "Library Service for People with Disabilities—Resources," for an annotated bibliography of publications.)

## STEP 1: GATHERING INFORMATION ABOUT THE ADA AND YOUR LIBRARY

Before decisions are made about changes to policy, procedures, and service delivery, library managers should become knowledgeable about the Americans with Disabilities Act (ADA) of 1990 to an extent that will enable them to conduct planning and implement needed changes. The preceding chapter provided information on the ADA, and it is strongly recommended that managers read the regulations for either Title II or Title III, as is appropriate to their situation, the ADA Accessibility Guidelines for Buildings and Facilities (ADAAG), and the regulations for Title I (Employment).

A number of articles and pamphlets have been published and are useful in understanding the ADA. Advocacy groups for people with disabilities and government agencies provide both published and telephone information services. For more information, see the first list of resources at the end of this chapter, "Americans with Disabilities Act—Resources," which provides a bibliography of publications about the ADA and a list of resources for gathering ADA-related information.

To obtain the full text of the Americans with Disabilities Act (ADA) of 1990 in alternate formats, contact: American Printing House for the Blind, Post Office Box 6085, Louisville, Kentucky 40206, Phone: (502) 895-2405. One copy of a Braille, large print, audiocassette, or flexible record is free. There is a nominal cost for additional copies.

It will not be sufficient to know about the law and regulations, however. Knowledge about the law will have to be applied to your library and the needs of your library users. Managers should consider these factors as they begin the planning process:

- What titles of the law are pertinent to your program? Title II (Public Services) applies to state and local entities; Title III to privately provided public accommodations, including libraries; Title I to all public employers and to private employers of a specified size.

- Is new construction or renovation under way or being considered? If so, does the law apply to that construction? For Title II, the law applies if construction started after January 26, 1992; for Title III, if constructed for first occupancy by January 26, 1993.

- Is the user group limited or open? Can you identify users with disabilities (remember that many disabilities are hidden, such as a heart or asthmatic condition), or is your user group so broad that a significant variety of needs must be addressed? The law defines disability very broadly; it has a functional, not a categorical definition. An individual who meets the tests defined in the regulations may not necessarily fall into a traditionally perceived disability type, such as the blind or wheelchair users. Additionally, individuals who have a temporary disability may be covered by the law.

- Did the library go through a self-evaluation process when the Rehabilitation Act of 1973 was passed, and are there any records of that work, or of decisions reached in the process? What are your current policies about service to individuals with disabilities? For example, your building may be accessible but not your collection or programs. You will look further at this in the self-evaluation phase of planning for ADA implementation. Records of previous planning and policy decisions can be a starting place for your ADA review.

- Is the library a public entity that must carry out the specific requirements of the law where a number of employees (usually 50) defines whether or not a requirement applies? Will the larger governing entity that operates the library, when there is one, be carrying out these requirements or should the library do that? You will need to read further in this chapter to answer these questions, but be aware that Section 35.104 of the Title II regulation says that a public entity is "Any state or local government; any department, agency, special purpose district, or other instrumentality of a state or states or local government; and, the National Railroad Passenger Corporation, and any commuter authority."[1]

## STEP 2: THE ADA COORDINATOR

Section 35.107 of the ADA regulation for state and local entities (28 *CFR* Part 35) requires that entities employing 50 or more people must designate a "responsible employee" who will coordinate information about the ADA.[2] The name, phone number, and office address of this person or persons must be made available to all interested individuals. This requirement is derived from the former Department of Health, Education, and Welfare (HEW) regulation for Section 504 of the Rehabilitation Act of 1973, and it makes good management sense.

Further on in this chapter, requirements for self-evaluation, public notice, and grievance procedures will be explained. An individual who can take leadership in carrying out these requirements and who can become very informed about the ADA will be needed. "The requirement for designation of a particular employee and dissemination of information about how to locate that employee helps to ensure that individuals dealing with large agencies are able to easily find a responsible person who is familiar with the requirements of the Act . . . and can communicate those requirements to other individuals in the agency who may be unaware of their responsibilities."[3] Identifying an individual as the ADA coordinator is one method of meeting this requirement.

An ADA coordinator who is serving as the designated responsible employee can also assume the role of manager of the library's efforts to understand the law and provide accessible library service. Ultimately, the role of the ADA coordinator or designated responsible employee will be defined by library management, but in the planning process described in this chapter, the ADA coordinator takes a leadership role. When following this model, it is suggested that a library manager look for an individual who has:

- Knowledge of the needs of individuals with disabilities;
- Knowledge of and experience in providing library services to individuals with disabilities;
- Sufficient authority and status within the organization to bring enough credibility to the planning project to get the job done; and,
- Strong organizational, planning, and interpersonal skills.

## STEP 3: SELF-EVALUATION

Section 35.105 of the ADA regulation for state and local entities requires that current policies and practices be evaluated to identify and correct any that are not consistent with the requirements of the regulations.[4] The regulation also states that public entities may have conducted such a self-evaluation under the requirements of the Rehabilitation Act of 1973, and, if so, these entities have to evaluate only those policies and practices not covered in the last self-evaluation. Clarification of this requirement in the *Federal Register* indicates, however, that public entities would be well advised to reexamine all of their policies and programs. Many services and materials found in libraries today were scarce or nonexistent 19 years ago, such as automated public access catalogs, database searching, and videocassettes.

> Programs and functions may have changed, and actions that were supposed to have been taken to comply with Section 504 may not have been fully implemented or may no longer be effective. In addition, there have been statutory amendments to Section 504 which have changed the coverage of Section 504, particularly the Civil Rights Restoration Act of 1987, Public Law No. 100-259, 102 Stat. 28 (1988), which broadened the definition of a covered "program or activity."[5]

The availability of new auxiliary aids that are used today by individuals with disabilities, especially personal computers and other electronic technology, is another reason for carrying out a full self-evaluation. These devices were not available when Section 504 self-evaluations were conducted and therefore were not considered options for improving access. Because so much of this new technology relates to the use of print material, it is especially critical that libraries review their practices to see how the new auxiliary aids can be incorporated into library service.

The *Federal Register* explains that conducting a self-evaluation during the one-year period allowed for compliance with this requirement does not change the effective date of the law. Public entities should be aware that they are not shielded from discrimination claims during that year. This information reinforces the need for a timely start and completion of the self-evaluation.

Documentation of a self-evaluation must be kept on file for at least three years (for entities that employ 50 or more people). The regulation prescribes that documentation must contain a list of the interested persons consulted, a description of areas examined and problems identified, and a description of modifications made.

The ADA coordinator in your library or library system can provide leadership in carrying out the self-evaluation, but there are other essential parties to this process. Individuals with disabilities who use or are interested in the library must be included.

> Experience has demonstrated the self-evaluation process to be a valuable means of establishing a working relationship with individuals

with disabilities, which has promoted both effective and efficient implementation of Section 504. The Department expects it will likewise be useful to public entities newly covered by the ADA.[6]

Libraries can use several methods for including people with disabilities in the process of reviewing facilities and services. A combination of methods will be the most useful and will assure that library managers collect the widest amount and variety of information on the needs of individuals with disabilities who want to use, or are currently using, their libraries. Several options are discussed later in this chapter.

A key to accessing individuals with disabilities is the advocacy or consumer group. These organizations, usually established as non-profit groups, advocate for services and rights for individuals with disabilities. They most often advocate for a single type of disability, and will include that disability in the name of their organization, such as the *American Council of the Blind* or the *Asthma and Allergy Foundation of America.* Other organizations advocate for all individuals with disabilities, such as *DREDF*, the *Disability Rights Education and Defense Fund.* See the third list of resources at the end of this chapter, "Organizations for People with Disabilities," for resources on advocacy organizations.

## Public Forums

Well-advertised public forums, where people can publicly speak their opinion and describe their service needs, are very helpful in developing a sense of what people want the library to do for them. Public forums are recommended as an early and recurring step in the process of information gathering because the information collected will be dependent upon who attends and so will be incomplete.

## Surveying Advocacy Groups and Library Consumers

Another approach for information gathering that provides consumers a single opportunity to speak out is the survey. A survey tool must be developed that will allow individuals with a great variety of conditions and needs to express those needs. It must also be phrased in such a way that an extensive knowledge of library functions and procedures is not required. And, lastly, it must be presented to many people who do not presently use the library. One avenue for presenting a survey to people who are not library users is through local groups that advocate for or serve individuals with disabilities. These organizations can disseminate a survey for you, or allow you to present it at their group meetings.

## Advisory Committee or Task Force

Establishing a group that can provide information and advice throughout the planning and implementation process is an effective method of including individuals with disabilities in this process. The group may take the form of an ad hoc task force of consumers, reporting its recommendations to library management, with the ADA coordinator providing staff support. Another option is a task force composed of both library staff and individuals with disabilities. The task force approach implies a relatively short-term function that has a set purpose and an anticipated date for completing the group's activity.

Library managers who are looking for advice and assistance over the long term may find an advisory committee to be more appropriate than a task force. In either case, discussion of the establishment of this group with the library's governing body will be necessary. Library management should have clearly in mind the role, mission, and objectives of any group appointed to assist in achieving compliance with the ADA and improving access to library services. As library managers approach their boards and governing agencies to establish such groups, they should also consider the need to ensure representation of persons with disabilities in the community on a continuing basis on all advisory and governing committees or boards.

Activities of advisory groups can include a regular schedule of meetings at which members review policies and procedures for areas of concern, conduct walk-throughs of the library to evaluate accessibility, advise on plans for public forums, review and comment on plans for implementation of accessible service, provide advice on auxiliary aids, review and provide advice on complaints about library service that are related to access for individuals with disabilities, and any number of other activities where they have expertise that the library manager and his or her staff lack.

## Identifying Consumers with Disabilities

As a first step in identifying individuals to serve on an advisory group, a list of local contact points can be assembled. Prospective group members who are citizens of the library's service community and who have a disability may be known to library management and therefore be easy to locate. These people may not, however, be fully representative of the range of disabilities and needs that should be considered, and appropriate people will have to be found through other channels. Resources for finding them are found in the third list of resources at the end of this chapter, "Organizations for People with Disabilities." Some simple suggestions for getting started are:

- Call the local chapters or branches of state and national advocacy groups for people with disabilities. Your local telephone book, along with the resources in the third list at the end of this chapter, "Organizations for People with Disabilities," are places to begin.

- Call the regional or district office of your state's human services and vocational rehabilitation agencies. Consult the telephone book under state agencies.

- Contact your local government's council, office, or committee on services to people with disabilities. Ask at the office of the mayor or the county administrator.

- Contact the regional library for the blind and physically handicapped in your state (or subregional in your area if there is one) that is a part of the *National Library Service for the Blind and Physically Handicapped Network*. A national directory is available free from the National Library Service for the Blind and Physically Handicapped, Library of Congress, Washington, DC, 20542.

### Communicating with Individuals with Disabilities

In keeping with the intent of the ADA to require full access to publicly and privately provided services, the regulations describe necessary communication efforts. Section 35.160 of the *Federal Register* describes the importance of ensuring that communications with individuals with disabilities are as effective as communications with other members of the public.[7] Subpart E—Communications, of the Title II regulation, requires that the public entity must furnish appropriate auxiliary aids and services for communication when necessary and that the entity must provide an opportunity for individuals with disabilities to request the auxiliary aids and services of their choice.[8]

Before a library even begins to assess the need for such devices and services for access to library service, it will have to do so for public forums and interactions with the members of advisory or similar groups. Auxiliary aids and services, such as assistive listening devices or sign language interpreters must be available to those who need them at meetings and presentations. Written communications will have to be adapted for individuals who are blind or have low vision, and that may require the use of audio recordings, electronic formats, large print, or Braille. Telephone conversations may require the use of a telecommunication device for the deaf (TDD). Meeting rooms must be fully accessible to persons who use wheelchairs or other mobility aids. Accommodations for guide or service animals must be made. It will be important to ask participants in your information gathering activities to inform you of their needs, so accommodations can be arranged in advance.

A further consideration related to communication is a concern that references to individuals with disabilities be made in a sensitive way. Disability advocacy groups and individuals with disabilities are insisting that they be referred to with dignity and respect, rather than with terminology that emphasizes their differences from others and is stereotyping. An example is the use of the phrase "individuals with disabilities," rather than "the disabled," "the handicapped," or other terms and phrases that make a disability appear to be the most important thing about a person. Referring to an individual's personhood first, rather than to a disability they have, is often called People First language.

Every publication about services to individuals with disabilities discusses this issue; for some in-depth reading, try these resources:

Dattilo, John and Smith, Ralph W. "Communicating Positive Attitudes Toward People with Disabilities Through Sensitive Terminology," *Therapeutic Recreation Journal*, First Quarter, 1990:8-17.
> Provides a history of the use of various terminology to refer to people with disabilities, suggested language preferred today, and a summary of existing debate and controversy surrounding some words and phrases.

Holmes, Gary E. and Karst, Ronald H. "The Institutionalization of Disability Myths: Impact on Vocational Rehabilitation Services," *Journal of Rehabilitation*, January/February/March, 1990.
> Explores ways in which disability myths become institutionalized, provides suggestions on how to prevent unknowingly incorporating disability myths into encounters with individuals with disabilities.

*Meeting and Introducing Persons with Disabilities*, a pamphlet available free from the National Easter Seal Society, 2023 West Ogden Avenue, Chicago, IL 60612.
> These guidelines have been compiled for all those who have occasion to meet persons with disabilities—or to introduce them to others. This is an excellent, brief introduction for people who have not had the

opportunity for much contact with persons with mobility, speech, hearing, and vision disabilities.

There is one further point to be made about identifying individuals who can tell library management what people with disabilities need to access a library. For many years disability advocacy groups have worked to promote their own disability-specific causes. Recent activities by these groups that focused on the passage of the ADA have been more coordinated and directed towards improving the life situation of all people with disabilities, not just the people who have a particular disability. That does not mean, however, that a blind person knows all about being deaf, or that a hearing impaired person can relate well to the needs of an individual who uses a wheelchair. Efforts to consult with people with disabilities should be carefully structured to assure that the opportunity is broadcast as widely as possible across the disability community. Using a combination of the approaches described above, and consulting with multiple advocacy groups, will help libraries reach a variety of people who have disabilities, but whose needs for accessing library service may be quite different from one another.

## Self-Evaluation Methods: What Should We Look At?

Most of the publications annotated in the second list of resources at the end of this chapter, "Library Service for People with Disabilities—Resources," have checklists and sections on "what should we look at?" Briefly, the major areas that library managers should review during the self-evaluation process are:

**Buildings and Facilities Access: Internal and External** — This includes, for example, accessible parking, entrances, thresholds, carpeting, doors, elevators, bathrooms, meeting rooms, water fountains; access to permanently installed equipment such as pay telephones, security systems, and card catalogs; access to furnishings, shelving, photocopiers, and vending machines; access to signage; access to outreach facilities such as bookmobiles; and access for children with disabilities as well as adults. This is not an exhaustive list; see the appropriate federal regulation on access to buildings and facilities for a thorough listing of requirements.

**Service Access** — This includes all the services provided by the library or library system, such as access to reference service (telephone and on-site); access to group programs presented by the library for children and adults, both those of general interest and those specific to the interests of the disability community; access to information and referral services;

access to a materials collection in accessible formats; access to materials that respond to information queries concerning disabilities; access to equipment used with library materials, such as CD/ROM and computers; access to the automated catalog; access to outreach programs and services. Again, this is not an exhaustive list. See the published resources on library service for persons with disabilities for comprehensive information.

**Policies and Procedures** — Published and unpublished, all library policies should be reviewed and revised as needed to assure that full and equal access for individuals with disabilities is provided.

**Staff Training** — Training the library staff, including volunteers, is a critical step for assuring equal access to service. The self-evaluation process should review current practice and needed change in this area. The inclusion of sensitivity and disability awareness training is particularly important to avoid excluding persons with disabilities because of stereotypical attitudes held by library staff. Beyond awareness training, the library must train staff to use auxiliary equipment that is available.

**Employment Practices** — Practices and policies for hiring, promotion, retention, and employee discipline and all other employment actions must be reviewed and revised as needed. Title I (Employment) of the ADA focuses on the ability of the individual to carry out the essential functions of a job, so employers will have to identify these for each job description. Volunteers are not covered by this title of the law.

## STEP 4: IMPLEMENTATION PLANNING

The self-evaluation process carried out to meet the requirements of the regulation and to assess current facilities, services, and practices for accessibility will result in the need for an implementation plan. As was stated earlier, the regulation for state and local entities requires that documentation of steps taken as a result of the self-evaluation plan be kept on file.

The program accessibility concept set forth in the regulation for Title II, Public Services, Subpart D, mandates a transition plan that requires structural modifications for entities that employ 50 or more persons. The plan must be developed within six months of the effective date of the regulation (January 26, 1992). This transition plan for needed structural changes could be incorporated into an overall transition plan that includes the self-evaluation activity, and all action required to comply with the requirements of the law, including changes to facilities, services, and policies. A simple format that lists action steps and substeps, responsible persons, and start and finish dates and that provides space for progress notes can be used to organize your planning and implementation activity. Some of the major action steps you will need to cover in your action plan are discussed here. Once again, this is not an exhaustive list.

## Continued Use of Consumers

The continued use of consumers during the implementation planning phase is highly recommended. They are an excellent source of information on the quality of various auxiliary aids and can provide product evaluations as you determine what equipment to purchase. Consumers will be able to help by looking for gaps in your review of services and facilities and by correcting misconceptions about what actions will provide accessible library services.

Consumer participation in the development of and review of transition plans can also go a long way toward assuring the disability community that you are serious in your effort to meet their needs and that you are actively working towards that goal. The regulations present specific time frames for planning and transition, but they do not protect the agency from claims of discrimination while this work is in progress. Consumer advisors can support the efforts of the library or library system if they believe in your good faith, and they can, armed with an understanding of your planning and implementation process, support your agency against claims of discrimination.

## Cooperation with Other Service Providers in Your Area and Governance Structure

As you carry out a self-evaluation and begin to see what changes need to be made, meet with other library service providers in your area to see where overlapping services can be made accessible in a coordinated way. You may find that a single, shared reading machine will be adequate to meet the need if there is an academic library very near your small public library that is willing to meet your patrons' need for this type of access to print materials. ADA coordinators, if this model for planning is used, can share ideas and resources to reduce both the cost of compliance with the ADA and the possibility of failure to provide accessible service.

The larger entity to which your organization belongs, whether a state or local government, or a large private organization, will also be evaluating services for accessibility. If your library or library system does not employ 50 or more people, but the overall governing body does, you may be carrying out these planning and implementation activities in concert with other representatives of that governing body, rather than on your own. This model can still be used, either by the larger governing body, or by the library as it brings information back to the larger planning group.

Clearly, any responsible manager will consult with his or her supervisor concerning this process, not only to inform them of the work in progress, but also to seek guidance on how to proceed. In so doing, it is hoped that activities related to the ADA that are going on in other sections of the larger organization will be discovered so the ADA coordinator can take advantage of such activity. Seeking cooperative efforts with other parts of the organization is an important action step for your library.

## Notice

Section 35.106 of the Title II regulation requires a public entity to disseminate sufficient information to applicants, participants, beneficiaries, and other interested persons to inform them of the rights and protections afforded by the ADA relative to the services of that entity.[9] Methods of providing this information include handbooks, manuals, and pamphlets that are distributed to the public to describe a public entity's programs and activities. Other suggested methods are posters in service locations and the broadcast of information by television or radio. The regulation reminds public entities that the required notice must be provided in accordance with the requirements for effective communication in Section 35.160 of the regulation.[10]

Libraries of all types typically produce pamphlets describing their services, hours of operation, and so forth. They also have user registration forms (applications). Information on special functions and programs, such as the summer library program, orientation to the library, or program presentations are also advertised, often through flyers or the local newspaper. Many libraries, especially those serving the general public, use television and radio to advertise services. The requirement for notice makes clear that all of these materials must describe how services are accessible as required by the ADA and that the notices themselves must be available in accessible formats, such as electronic disc, Braille, sound recordings, and captioned video.

## Grievance Procedures

Section 35.107 of the Title II regulations, the section that requires the designation of a responsible employee (or ADA coordinator in this planning model), also requires that employers of 50 or more persons must adopt grievance procedures for resolving complaints.[11] The grievance procedure should be a mechanism for resolution of complaints at the local level. Individuals covered by the law have the right to file complaints with a federal enforcement agency and in the courts as provided for by the law, but they should inform the entity about their complaint before going to higher authorities. They can, however, file complaints with higher authorities before having exhausted the grievance procedure of the state or local entity.

Most local and state libraries have a grievance procedure in place, but it may not cover the complaints of individuals with disabilities. Privately operated libraries should also consider establishing a grievance procedure for their users, if they do not already have one.

## Specific Areas of Service and Methods of Service Delivery

This component of your plan should be the most extensive, because it covers the work of determining how everything that the library does will be addressed in terms of accessibility for individuals with disabilities. It is well worth the investment to get copies of some of the titles described in the second resource list at the end of this chapter, "Library Service for People with Disabilities—Resources." Without formal training in rehabilitation services or other human service professions, librarians must rely on the expertise of others. A number of excellent resources have been published.

This component of your action plan should also carefully address the financial resources needed to carry out the needed activities and purchases. Financial planning may include grant applications for Library Services and Construction Act (LSCA) funds, or other types of grant funding. LSCA has two funding categories that specifically address services to people with disabilities: Physically Handicapped, for services to individuals who are unable to use print, and Handicapped, for services to any person with disabilities.

Library managers should not limit their search for funding to grant applications, however. The requirement for providing accessible services is now the law of the land and state and local entities are responsible for meeting the obligation. Preparing budget requests for necessary renovations or purchase of auxiliary aids and services, for the costs of staff training, and other activities is a part of the planning process.

## Auxiliary Aids and Services

Plans for making specific areas of service and methods of service delivery accessible must include the provision of auxiliary aids and services. Aids and services are an important part of the provision of accessible library service because so many of them are used to make print and voice delivered information accessible, so your action plan may need to address them separately. Auxiliary aids and services include a wide range of services and devices for ensuring effective communication and delivery of information. The Title II and Title III regulations do not provide complete catalogs of such aids and services, but, instead, suggest examples. The fourth resource at the end of this chapter, "Auxiliary Aids," provides resources for complete lists of aids and lists of vendors, resources for information on the types of equipment available, and resources for lists of agencies that provide services related to the auxiliary aids and services.

The publications on library services for individuals with disabilities included in the resource list, "Auxiliary Aids," are also very helpful in explaining how various auxiliary aids are used in libraries. Do not forget the expertise of your consumers with disabilities as you look at auxiliary aids. Many of them have had experience with this equipment and their assessments of quality can prevent costly purchasing errors.

Auxiliary aids and services are used to overcome visual, hearing, speech, and physical limitations and are often referred to as assistive devices. Examples of assistive devices used by people with disabilities and that can be used to make your library services accessible include (but are not limited to):

**Computers** — Perhaps the single most useful tool, because it allows so many other tools to work.

**Speech Synthesizer** — Also called voice output, the speech synthesizer reads print aloud. It has obvious uses for online catalogs, other electronically stored information, and individual use of print materials in the library. OCR (Optical Character Recognition) technology can scan the information on a page and transform it into audible information to work with printed text.

**Software** — Special software is needed to use some of the computer adaptations available.

**Switches** — A device that operates another device; can be used with computers to enable people with physical limitations to operate an online catalog or access other materials that are stored electronically.

**Voice Recognition** — A computer has the ability to recognize voice commands.

**Touch-Sensitive Display** — Allows the user to operate a computer by touching the screen instead of using a keyboard.

**Page Turners** — Electric or mouth-held, these enable a person with physical limitations to use a book or other printed material.

**Large or Magnified Print** — Familiar to librarians in print format and also available electronically. The computer monitor presents large print displays of information (Enlarged Display enlarges pictures and text; Large Print Display just does text.) Other devices, such as closed circuit TVs (CCTV) and glass magnifiers can provide enlargement of printed material.

**Alternate Materials Formats** — These include Braille, audio recordings, electronically stored, large print, captioned video, and others. Libraries, since they manage and provide access to information, need to provide that access in alternate formats.

**Amplification** — Whether of the meeting room sound system, during the reference inquiry process, at the information or circulation desk, or in any of the interactions in a library that require hearing, amplification can be used to make service accessible. Assistive listening devices for meeting rooms and personal conversations are the primary tool used. Videotext, where spoken information immediately appears on a screen or video monitor, is a growing option.

**Telecommunication Devices for the Deaf (TDD)** — also called text telephones, TDDs allow telephone use by presenting a printed or electronic display, instead of a voice, over the phone. Many people in the deaf community use them, and the ADA regulations say they should be available at public libraries, at least for telephone reference service.

**Electronic Speech Aids** — Any one of a number of devices which allow individuals with speech limitations to have conversations, write and store messages, and have access to computers. An example for library use is a small device that accepts typed text and displays it electronically. The electronic readout enables a person without speech to communicate quickly and effectively at an information or reference desk.

**Technical Aids** — Devices, such as keyguards and keylocks, that enable a person with a disability to operate a computer.

**Braille Embossers/Printers** — Text that is stored electronically can be produced in Braille, or printed text can be scanned into electronic form in preparation for production in Braille.

These general categories give some idea of the variety and depth of assistive devices available. As you consider their use in your library, also consider how they can be used to accommodate the needs of a prospective or existing employee.

## Employment

A major purpose of the ADA is to enable individuals with disabilities to join the workforce. The technology is available to accommodate their needs and the law requires employers, both public and private, to make that technology available. Tax credits are even available for tax-paying employers who spend money to accommodate an employee's need. The ADA also discusses discrimination in employment because of negative attitudes and stereotypes about individuals with disabilities and makes the employer responsible for overcoming this kind of discrimination. Title I, Employment, does not tell an employer how to provide accommodations, just that it must be done within reason.

Payne & Associates, in Olympia, Washington, uses a model for assisting human resource managers to determine and provide needed workplace accommodations for individuals with learning disabilities (from a handout provided at the 1991 National Association for Adults with Special Learning Needs Annual Conference in Vienna, Virginia). The model consists of four steps: 1. assessment, 2. planning, 3. implementation, and 4. evaluation. This is, of course, a basic model for problem resolution, and it is applicable to any situation where an eligible applicant (one that can, with or without reasonable accommodation, carry out the essential job functions) is employed or being considered for employment.

Basically, the model requires that the employee/applicant, the employer or supervisor, and the coworkers of the employee/applicant apply problem solving techniques to determine what reasonable accommodations will work. According to Payne, this team approach works because it gives everyone concerned an opportunity to express their issues and, after discussion, to buy into the solutions agreed upon.

Often, reasonable accommodations may be very simple and straightforward, such as providing a CCTV or amplification on the telephone instrument. But acceptance and understanding by coworkers and supervisors must be gained if the employee with a disability is to have a successful work experience, even if it is the law to provide the accommodation.

## STEP 5: IMPLEMENTATION

The next step in this planning model requires that the plans developed as a result of a self-evaluation and study of possible methods of making services accessible be carried out. The titles listed in the annotated bibliography in the second resource list, "Library Services for People with Disabilities—Resources," will again be very useful to library managers. They provide extensive how-to information, references, and resources. Some of the resources in the third resource list, "Organizations for People with Disabilities," will also be helpful in implementing your plans.

If the library manager is not burned out on developing plans at this point, another one may be useful. This plan should emphasize the time frames within which activities will be carried out and when various facets of the accessibility implementation will be completed and available to the library user. The plan should also address public relations related to the project, what forms public relations efforts will take, and how the disability community will be informed that the library is becoming fully accessible.

## STEP 6: CONTINUING ACCESSIBLE SERVICE

Section 35.133 to the Title II regulations discusses maintenance of accessible features. Features of facilities and equipment that are required to be readily accessible to and usable by persons with disabilities, as required by the ADA and the regulation, must be maintained in good working condition.[12] In other words, it is not enough to provide such features as accessible elevators, ramps, and routes; a public entity must keep those features in working order and available to the public.

While this section of the regulation specifically discusses accessible facilities and features, it is reasonable to assume that public entities should also maintain the accessibility to services, as well as to buildings and facilities. Library managers must begin to think in terms of the issue of access to their program as a part of all planning for and provision of library service, and they must do so continuously, not just during the self-evaluation or change implementation period.

Again, the consumer will be a most helpful resource to the library manager in assuring the continuation of accessible services. Appointing consumers with disabilities to ongoing governing and advisory boards is a step towards gaining a continuing evaluation of access to library services by individuals with disabilities.

The many approaches to assessing quality of library service can also be used to assess the quality of service to people with disabilities. Usually, these methods, such as periodic need, usage, and satisfaction with service surveys, solicit consumer input. Every such survey should include questions about service to people with disabilities, including questions about the physical facilities, the availability of equipment, access to materials in the needed formats and on the desired topics, and access to appropriate programming for people with disabilities. Such survey questions will give people with disabilities the opportunity to give continuous suggestions, complaints, and service ideas to library management.

## SUMMARY

Two recurring themes emerge from this discussion of a planning model that libraries can use in implementing the requirements of the Americans with Disabilities Act (ADA) of 1990. The first is that listening to consumers who have disabilities is critical in the planning process and in the ongoing provision of service. The second is that there are a lot of resources available to help library planners decide what needs to be done, how to do it, and where to get help doing it.

Listening to consumers should not be new to library managers. Certainly, for public libraries at least, the Public Library Association publication *OutPut Measures for Public Libraries* strongly encourages that type of success measurement. The bottom line is this: Do we meet your needs? If not, how can we meet your needs? This model encourages the library manager to assume the posture of asking consumers those questions at the beginning of planning, during implementation, and on into the future.

The resource lists that follow provide information on organizations and available publications. Most organizations have free long-distance telephone access; publications are often free or inexpensive. Call them up, write for their publications, and keep the responses on hand for your staff and for library users. There is really very little that you cannot find out about the library service needs of people with disabilities, and about the means to meet those needs, through these resources.

# REFERENCES

1. 56 *Federal Register* 35697.
2. 56 *Federal Register* 35702.
3. Ibid.
4. 56 *Federal Register* 35701.
5. 56 *Federal Register* 35702.
6. 56 *Federal Register* 35701.
7. 56 *Federal Register* 35711-12.
8. Ibid.
9. 56 *Federal Register* 35702.
10. 56 *Federal Register* 35711.
11. 56 *Federal Register* 35702.
12. 56 *Federal Register* 35707.

# AMERICANS WITH DISABILITIES ACT—RESOURCES

## Organizations

For information on the ADAAG guidelines for buildings and facilities contact:

**Architectural and Transportation Barriers Compliance Board**
1111 18th Street, NW, Suite 501
Washington, DC 20036
Voice: (800) USA-ABLE; TDD: (800) USA-ABLE

For information on ADA requirements affecting transportation

**Department of Transportation**
400 Seventh Street, SW
Washington, DC 20590
Voice: (202) 366-9305; TDD: (202) 755-7687

DREDF has established an ADA training unit that offers indepth legal and technical training, workshops and conference speakers, and training materials.

**The Disability Rights Education and Defense Fund, Inc. (DREDF)**
2212 Sixth Street
Berkeley, CA 94710
Voice: (415) 644-2555; TDD: (415) 644-2629; FAX: (415) 841-8645

1616 P Street, Suite 100
Washington, DC 20036
Voice or TDD: (202) 986-0375; (800) 466-4ADA (Hotline funded by
Department of Justice)

For information on Title I (Employment) contact:

**Equal Employment Opportunity Commission (EEOC)**
1801 L Street, NW
Washington, DC 20507
Voice: (800) USA-EEOC; TDD: (800) 800-3302

For information on ADA requirements affecting telecommunications
contact:

**Federal Communications Commission (FCC)**
1919 M Street, NW
Washington, DC 20554
Voice: (202) 634-1837; TDD: (202) 632-1836

**Internal Revenue Service (IRS)**
Office of the Chief Counsel
CC:PSI:6
1111 Constitution Avenue, NW
Room 5111
Washington, DC 20224
Voice: (202) 566-3292

**National Council on Disability**
800 Independence Avenue, SW, Suite 814
Washington, DC 20591
Voice: (202) 267-3846; TDD: (202) 267-3232; FAX: (202) 453-4240

For information on the requirements of Title II (Public Services) and
Title III (Public Accommodations) and to get free informational
materials contact:

**Office on the Americans with Disabilities Act**
Civil Rights Division, U.S. Department of Justice
Post Office Box 66118
Washington, DC 20035-6118
Voice: (202) 514-0301; TDD: (202) 514-0381 or (202) 514-0383; Elec-
tronic Bulletin Board: (202) 514-6193

## Books, Pamphlets, Reports, Videos

*ADA: A Summary of the Law and Its Impact on People with Mental Disabilities,* National Mental Health Association. $5.00. Order from NMHA, 1021 Prince St., Alexandria, VA 22314.

*ADA: An Analysis,* Business Publishers, Inc. $12.95, prepaid. Order from BPI, 951 Pershing Dr., Silver Spring, MD 20910.

*ADA: An Easy Checklist,* National Easter Seal Society. $.75 each, plus $.65 postage. Order from National Easter Seal Society, 70 E. Lake St., Chicago, IL 60601. Publication E-69.

*ADA: An Opportunity for All,* National Association of Rehabilitation Facilities. $.50. Order from NARF, P.O. Box 17675, Washington, DC 20041.

*The ADA and HIV: What Employers Need to Know Now,* National Leadership Coalition on AIDS. $5.00. Order from the Coalition, 1150 17th St., NW, Suite 202, Washington, DC 20036.

*ADA Compliance Guide.* Thompson Publishing Group. Order from Thompson Publishing Group, 1725 N. Salisbury Blvd., Salisbury, MD 21801-0330. $198.00 per year for the guide and monthly news bulletins.

*ADA Management Kit,* Mainstream, Inc. $39.95. Order from Mainstream, P. O. Box 65183, Washington, DC 20035.

"ADA Update: Justice, EEOC Issues Proposed ADA Rules," *Handicapped Requirements Handbook,* Supplement Number 148, March 1991. Request from the Federal Programs Advisory Service, Thompson Publishing Group, 1725 K St., NW, Suite 200, Washington, DC, 20006.

*Americans with Disabilities Act Handbook,* U.S. EEOC and Department of Justice, October 1991. Available free to libraries from the EEOC or DOJ.

*The Americans with Disabilities Act: A Practical & Legal Guide to Impact, Enforcement and Compliance,* 1990, Bureau of National Affairs, Inc. (BNA), BNA Book Distribution Center, 300 Raritan Center Parkway, PO Box 7816, Edison, NJ 08818.

*The Americans with Disabilities Act: An Overview, 1990.* Available free of charge from the Texas Young Lawyers Association, P.O. Box 12487, Austin, TX, 78711.

*The Americans with Disabilities Act: Questions and Answers,* U.S. Department of Justice, Civil Rights Division, Office on the ADA, 1991. Request from the Office on the ADA, P.O. Box 66118, Washington, DC, 20035-6118. GLPOO: 1991 0-290-205

*The Americans with Disabilities Act: What It Means for People Living with AIDS*, American Civil Liberties Union, AIDS Project, ADA Education Project, 1991. Free from the ACLU Foundation National Headquarters, 132 W. 43rd St., New York, NY 10036.

Esposito, Michael, *Employment Action Steps for the Americans with Disabilities Act*. Free from Blank, Rome, Comisky & McCautey, Fort Penn Center Plaza, Philadelphia, PA 19103.

*Americans with Disabilities Act of 1990: Law and Explanation*, Commerce Clearing House, Inc. $10.00. Call (800) 248-3248 to order. Catalog # 4998.

Fasman, Zachary D., Mary C. Dollarhide, and Jeffrey M. Hahn, *What Business Must Know about the Americans with Disabilities Act*, U.S. Chamber of Commerce. Order from the U.S. Chamber of Commerce, Resources Policy Department, 1615 H St., NW, Washington, DC 20062. Publication #0230.

*Handicapped Requirements Handbook*, Thompson Publishing Group, $147.00 per year, 2 vol., loose-leaf monthly update. Order from Thompson Publishing Group, 1725 N. Salisbury Blvd., Salisbury, MD 21801-0330.

*Library Resources on the Employment of Individuals with Disabilities*, U.S. Equal Employment Opportunity Commission Library, November 1990. Free. Order from the U.S. Equal Employment Opportunity Commission Library, 1801 L St., NW, Washington, DC 20507.

*Nobody is Burning Wheelchairs*, National Easter Seal Society. Video, 15 mins. #35 from the Administrative Services Department of the National Easter Seal Society.

*REG FACTS, #1-13*, U.S. Department of Justice, Civil Rights Division, Office on the ADA, 1991. Request from the Office on the ADA, P.O. Box 66118, Washington, DC 20035-6118.

*Taking Care of Business*, Texas Rehabilitation Commission. Free copies are available from ADA-Texas, 4900 N. Lamar Blvd., Austin, TX 78751-2316 (telephone 483-4761 in Austin; (800) 442-9502 outside Austin).

*Technical Assistance Paper on Accessibility Codes and Standards*, U.S. Architectural and Transportation Compliance Board. Free. ATBCB, Suite 501, 1111 18th St., NW, Washington, DC 20036-3894.

Trowers-Crowley, S., *ADA Primer: A Concise Guide to the Americans with Disabilities Act of 1990*. Maxwell Macmillan, Front and Brown Sts., Riverside, NJ 08075, (800) 275-5755. 1990.

*Understanding the ADA*, Eastern Paralyzed Veterans Association. Free. Order from EPVA, 75-20 Astoria Blvd., Jackson Heights, NY 11370.

## Articles

Brown, Barbara Berish, "Washington Scene," *Employment Relations Today,* Vol. 17, No. 3, Autumn, 1990, pp. 243-48.

Dalton, Phyllis I., "Productivity, Not Paternalism," *Library Personnel News,* Vol. 4, No. 3, Summer, 1990, pp. 42-43.

Geber, Beverly, "The Disabled: Ready, Willing & Able," *Training,* Vol. 27, No. 12, December, 1990, pp. 29-36.

Goldman, Charles D., Esq., "Legal Access Beyond ADA: Which Way?" *The Braille Forum,* September-October, 1990, pp. 15-17.

Gunde, Michael G., "What Every Librarian Should Know About the Americans with Disabilities Act," *American Libraries,* Vol. 22, No. 8, September, 1991, pp. 806-09.

Gunde, Michael G. "Working with the Americans with Disabilities Act," *Library Journal,* Vol. 116, No. 21, December, 1991, p. 99.

Hunsicker, J.F., "Ready or Not: The ADA," *Personnel Journal,* Vol. 69, No. 8, August, 1990, pp. 80-86.

"Investing in America's Future," *Paraplegia News,* October, 1990, pp. 29-37.

Lewis, Christopher, "Americans with Disabilities Act," *LIBRARY ACCESS: Services for People with Disabilities,* Vol. 1, No. 1, January, 1991, pp. 1-3.

Lindsay, Ronald A., "Discrimination Against the Disabled: The Impact of the New Legislation," *Employee Relations Law Journal,* Vol. 15, No. 3, Winter, 1989, pp. 333-45.

McKee, Bradford E., "Planning for the Disabled," *Nation's Business,* Vol. 78, No. 11, November, 1990, pp. 24-26.

Murphy, Betty, "ADA Signed into Law," *Personnel Journal,* Vol. 69, No. 9, September, 1990, pp. 18-20.

Noel, Rita T., "Employing the Disabled: A How and Why Approach," *Training & Development Journal,* August, 1990, pp. 26-32.

Norlin, Dennis, "Spotlight: The Americans with Disabilities Act," *The Southeastern Librarian,* Winter, 1990, p. 175.

O'Donnell, Ruth, "The Americans with Disabilities Act," *Florida Libraries,* Vol. 34, No. 5, May, 1991, pp. 6-8.

Peak, Martha G., "Are You Ready for ADA?" *Personnel,* Vol. 68, No. 8, August, 1991, pp. 14-15.

"Special ADA Issue," *In the Mainstream,* Vol. 15, No. 4, July-August, 1990.

"Special Report," *Personnel Manager's Letter*, August 13, 1990.

Stone, Rocky, "Putting 'You' in the ADA Picture," *SHHH Journal*, November/ December, 1990, pp. 8-10.

Susser, Peter A., "The ADA: Dramatically Expanded Federal Rights for Disabled Americans," *Employee Relations Law Journal*, Vol. 16, No. 2, Autumn, 1990, pp. 157-76.

Thornburgh, Richard, "The Americans with Disabilities Act and the Future for Children," *Execptional Parent*, Vol. 21, No. 2, March, 1991, pp. W8-W10.

Tucker, Bonnie P., "The Americans with Disabilities Act: An Overview," *University of Illinois Law Review*, Vol. 1989, No. 4, pp. 923-39.

"What the New Disability Law Means to Office Telephone Users," *Creative Secretary's Letter*, September 19, 1990, pp. 6-7.

Williams, John M. and Chet Nagle, "The ADA: An Analysis—What Will the Americans with Disabilities Act Mean to You?" *Careers & the Disabled*, Vol. 6, No. 2, Spring, 1991, pp. 63-70.

*Worklife: A Publication on Employment and People with Disabilities*, Vol. 3, No. 3, Fall, 1990. (Special issue on the ADA.)

# LIBRARY SERVICE FOR PEOPLE WITH DISABILITIES— RESOURCES

## Books and Pamphlets

Baskin, Barbara H. and Karen H. Harris, eds. *The Mainstreamed Library: Issues, Ideas, Innovations*. Chicago: American Library Association, 1982.
Sections on the physical environment, materials selection, technology, software, program and outreach, with a focus on services to students in the educational setting and public library services to children and youth. Each section contains articles from the library and education literature; some articles are written by architects, therapists, and other professionals who work with individuals with disabilities. Other articles are original to this book and discuss innovative library programs. Indexed.

Cassell, Marianne Kotch and the Vermont Board of Libraries Access Task Force. *Planning for Accessibility*. Montpelier, VT: Department of Libraries, 1991.
The Vermont Department of Libraries developed this loose-leaf manual to assist Vermont libraries as they evaluate their buildings for accessibility under the Americans with Disabilities Act of 1990. The four sections on 1. Planning for Accessibility, 2. Getting Into the Library, 3. Using the

Library, and 4. Behind the Scenes suggest what to check and provide information on the requirements for compliance. Lists of resources, bibliographies, and a glossary are provided. Copies of the manual are available for loan from the Vermont Department of Libraries.

Dalton, Phyllis I. *Library Service to the Deaf and Hearing Impaired.* Phoenix, AZ: Oryx Press, 1985.

Very comprehensive coverage of such topics as deafness and hearing impairment, involving the deaf community, planning service delivery, and service provision. The 10 appendices provide a depth of information, including lists of agencies and resources, public relations strategies and materials, population statistics, and other useful items. A glossary and index are included.

Davis, Emmett A. and Catherine M. Davis. *Mainstreaming: Library Service for Disabled People.* Metuchen, NJ: Scarecrow Press, 1980.

The introduction and first chapter of this book present a discussion of attitudes about the disabled and the terms in the library catalog that are used to describe them. An extensive analysis of subject headings and the stereotypical attitudes toward individuals with disabilities that they portray is helpful in addressing this problem in libraries. A bibliography of print and film/video resources is provided.

Dequin, Henry C. *Librarians Serving Disabled Children and Young People.* Littleton, CO: Libraries Unlimited, 1983.

Some of the practical information in this book is out of date because of the development of new technology since it was published, but the lists of resources, methods for materials evaluation, and bibliographies remain useful. Indexed.

Florida Department of State, Division of Library and Information Services. *Library Services for Persons Who Are Mentally Retarded: Guidelines.* Tallahassee, FL: 1987.

Intended for public librarians, this brief guide is available free from the State Library of Florida. Bibliography, resource lists, and program suggestions are included.

Lovejoy, Eunice. *Portraits of Library Service to People with Disabilities.* Boston: G.K. Hall, 1990.

Through site visits to 19 public libraries and libraries for the blind and physically handicapped, the author collected information on library service to individuals with disabilities in a variety of settings. Special needs centers, outreach services, mobile services, and integrated services are presented along with several programs of the National Library Service for the Blind and Physically Handicapped. The appendix includes samples of public relations materials, a glossary and resource lists, and forms used in the library programs included in the book. The resource lists cover organizations, assistive equipment, and vendors of library materials.

Lucas, Linda and Marilyn H. Karrenbrock. *The Disabled Child in the Library: Moving into the Mainstream.* Littleton, CO: Libraries Unlimited, 1983.
   An introduction to disabilities of many types. Other sections discuss the needs of children for library service and information; materials, formats, and equipment that can be used; and services and programs that public libraries can provide for children with disabilities, their families, and advocates. The final chapter discusses environments. Bibliography and index. This book can be used as a text or a reference tool.

Marshall, Margaret R. *Libraries and the Handicapped Child.* Boulder, CO: Westview Press, 1981.
   Presents suggestions for service in public, school, and institutional libraries. Four chapters are organized according to disability type, with others focusing on the school library, the public library, toy libraries, storytelling, materials, and equipment. Appendices have resource lists and a bibliography. Indexed.

National Association for the Deaf, FOLDA-USA. *Communicating with Hearing People: The Red Notebook.* Silver Spring, MD. Annual updates.
   *The Red Notebook* is the popular name for this loose-leaf publication about deafness and services for deaf people. Includes resources, information on public and private agencies, and other vital reference material on the topic, as well as suggestions for library service.

National Library Service for the Blind and Physically Handicapped. *Planning Barrier Free Libraries.* Washington, DC: Library of Congress, 1981.
   Now that the new accessibility guidelines (ADAAG) are published, some of this information is dated. However, this planning guide for establishing a library for the blind and physically handicapped has some very good suggestions for barrier free design and includes an Accessibility Checklist.

National Library Service for the Blind and Physically Handicapped, Library of Congress, 1291 Taylor St., NW, Washington, DC 20542.
   NLS publishes Reference Circulars with information and resources on library services to persons with disabilities which are available from the National Library Service or your Regional Library for the Blind and Physically Handicapped. Some of the more useful of the circulars are: *Building a Library Collection on Blindness and Physical Disabilities: Basic Materials and Resources* (1990); *Guide to Spoken-Word Recordings: Foreign-Language Instruction and Literature* (1988); *Guide to Spoken-Word Recordings: Popular Literature* (1987); *Reading Materials in Large Type* (1987); *Reference Books in Special Media* (1982); and *Sources of Braille Reading Materials* (1985).

Sorenson, Liene S. *Accessible Library Services: Taking Action to Enhance Public Library Services for Persons with Disabilities.* Skokie, IL: Skokie Public Library, 1988. Order from the PLA Order Department, American Library Association, Chicago.

This manual is the result of three years of active work by the Skokie Public Library to enhance services to persons with disabilities. Chapters include information on planning and preparation, awareness and sensitivity, resources, services to children, technology, publicity and outreach, and much more. Although only 52 pages long, this inexpensive manual ($13.00; $10.00 to PLA members) is very useful and full of information.

Thomas, James L. and Carol H. Thomas, eds. *Library Services for the Handicapped Adult.* Phoenix, AZ: Oryx Press, 1982.

The resource lists and some of the service information in this book are out of date, but some of the reprinted articles provide service ideas and descriptions of the needs of individuals that continue to be valid.

Velleman, Ruth A. *Meeting the Needs of People with Disabilities: A Guide for Librarians, Educators, and Other Service Professionals.* Phoenix, AZ: Oryx Press, 1990.

Velleman's original book, *Serving Physically Disabled People: An Information Handbook for All Libraries,* has been revised and retitled. The result is a comprehensive and encyclopedic handbook of information for persons and agencies who provide services to individuals with disabilities. The book can also be used as a reference tool by anyone with a disability who is seeking answers to questions about available community resources and accessibility issues. The index is lengthy and contributes to the reference value of this work.

Wright, Kieth C. *Serving the Disabled: A How-To-Do-It Manual for Librarians.* Neal-Schuman, 1991.

The latest of Wright's books on this subject covers making library facilities accessible to those with physical disabilities, adapting the workplace, integrating special materials into the collection, and developing programs and services for individuals with disabilities. An introductory chapter discusses a definition of disabled and stereotypical attitudes about people with disabilities.

Wright, Kieth C. and Judith F. Davie. *Library and Information Services for Handicapped Individuals.* 3rd ed. Englewood, CO: Libraries Unlimited, 1989.

The third edition of this book adds information on staff training activities, the impact of technology, and contagious disease as a disability. Seven chapters describe specific types of disability conditions and adaptations to traditional service that can be used to make libraries fully accessible for individuals who have those conditions. An introductory chapter discusses disabilities in general, and the closing chapter concentrates on technology. Resource lists are provided. Indexed. This is an excellent handbook for the front line service provider and those who are training library staff.

Wright, Kieth C. and Judith F. Davie. *Library Manager's Guide to Hiring and Serving Disabled Persons.* Jefferson, NC: McFarland, 1990.

The authors have moved away from the individual librarian developing services for library users with disabilities and towards the library manager who has the means and responsibility to develop services to people with disabilities. Chapters cover staff development; recruiting, selecting, and hiring disabled persons; selection and acquisition of materials; organizing the library collection for accessibility; making the library facility accessible; information services; and public service programs. Thorough resource lists are provided. Indexed. This is a must buy for library managers who are working on compliance with the Americans with Disabilities Act of 1990.

## Video Resources

*Access: Services for the Blind and Physically Handicapped.* 20 mins., color. University of Denver, 1976.
    An overview of the Library of Congress National Library Service for the Blind and Physically Handicapped program.

*Access: Serving Disabled Persons in the Library.* 15 mins., color. Greater Vancouver Library Federation and the National Library of Canada, n.d.
    People with disabilities (mobility impairment, deafness, hearing impairment, blindness, visual impairment) describe their library needs, the barriers that prevent them from successfully using the library, and possible solutions to these barriers, including some auxiliary aids.

*First Florida Biennial Conference on Library Services for Persons with Handicaps* (1989) and *Second Florida Biennial Conference on Library Services for Persons with Disabilities* (1991). Copies of tapes will be made free of charge onto your blank VHS tape by the Florida Division of Blind Services, Bureau of Library Services for the Blind and Physically Handicapped, 420 Platt St., Daytona Beach, FL 32114-2804.
    Contents of the 1989 tapes include Call to Order; Community Resources for Persons with Hearing Impairments; Information Needs of People with Physical Disabilities; Involving Consumers in the Planning Process; Library Services to Children with Disabilities; Model Public Library Programs; Public Library Services to Visually Disabled Persons; The Role of Advocacy in Libraries; Talking Book Deposit Collections in Public Libraries; Training Library Staff to Work with Patrons with Special Needs; You've Got What It Takes: Service to Persons Who Are Developmentally Disabled.
    Contents of the 1991 tapes: The Americans with Disabilities Act of 1990: Implications for Libraries; Reading Never Sounded So Good: A Case Study in Public Relations for Talking Book Libraries; Call to Order; The Information Age and People with Disabilities: Attitudes, Advances, Access; Model Library Programs for People with Disabilities; Extending Library Service to Children with Disabilities: The Basics and Beyond; A

Joint Venture in Library Access for Special Populations: The Public Library and the National Library Service; Talking Book Deposit Collections in Florida; The Americans with Disabilities Act: Time for Action; Consumer Forum on Library Services to People with Disabilities.

*People First: Serving and Employing People with Disabilities.* VHS and 3/4" U-matic formats, 38 mins., color. Library Video Network, Baltimore County Public Library. Available from ALA Video, 50 E. Huron St., Chicago, IL.

An excellent staff training and awareness tool. People with disabilities are seen using libraries and describing what they need to access public library services. This video is useful not only for training library staff, but also for circulation to public organizations and local agencies.

*A Place Where I Belong: Serving Disabled Children in the Library.* 19 mins., color. Greater Vancouver Library Federation and the National Library of Canada, n.d.

Provides ideas to enable library staff to open their library to children with disabilities and includes suggested methods for special format materials, storytelling, and puppet shows.

*Sensitivity to the Disabled Person.* 29 mins., color. Library Video Network, Baltimore County Public Library, 1982.

People with disabilities are seen using libraries and describing what they need to access public library services. Similar in format to the *People First* video.

*They Just Want Into Whatever's Going On.* VHS, 20 mins., color. Summer Institute on Library Services for Youth with Disabilities, Indiana University, 1990.

Introduces the philosophy of integrated service for school and public library programs for young people with disabilities. Practical ideas from librarians are offered, along with advice from published experts. Kids are shown in integrated library settings with their nondisabled peers. This video is a very useful tool for staff training and awareness sessions.

# INFORMATION ORGANIZATIONS FOR PEOPLE WITH DISABILITIES

**ACCESS ERIC,** 1920 Association Dr., Reston, VA 22091, Voice: (800) 873-3742.

A unit of the Educational Resources Information Center (ERIC) established to answer questions about ERIC services and components and how to use ERIC resources.

**National Clearinghouse on Women and Girls with Disabilities,** Educational Equity Concepts, Inc., 114 East 32 St., New York, NY 10016, (212) 725-1803.

This group publishes *Bridging the Gap: A National Directory of Services for Women and Girls with Disabilities,* which contains 300 listings of agencies and organizations in the U.S. and Canada.

**National Information Center for Children and Youth with Handicaps,** P.O. Box 1492, Washington, DC 20013, Voice: (800) 999-5599; TDD: (703) 893-8614.

Free publications on national, state, and regional resources. Also provides referrals, prepared information packets, publications, and technical assistance.

**National Rehabilitation Information Center (NARIC),** 8455 Colesville Road, Suite 935, Silver Spring, MD 20910-3319.

NARIC is a library and information center on disability and rehabilitation. Provides a variety of information services, including ABLEDATA, a products database. NARIC publishes the *NARIC Guide to Disability and Rehabilitation Periodicals,* $15.00, which lists publications by category. Indexed by subject.

**Recording for the Blind (RFB),** 20 Rosel Road, Princeton, NJ 05540, Voice: (609) 452-0606.

RFB provides lists of recording studios across the nation and recorded textbooks, library services, and other educational resources to people who cannot use standard print.

## Publications

*AAD/Reference 1990,* Vol. 135, No. 2., pp. 165-83.

Provides lists of federal agencies, state vocational rehabilitation offices, professional organizations, and regional/local programs.

"Annual Directory of National Organizations, 1991-92." *Exceptional Parent,* September, 1991.

*Blindness and Visual Impairments: National Information and Advocacy Organizations,* 1990. National Library Service for the Blind and Physically Handicapped, Library of Congress, Washington, DC 20542.

Lists organizations and other publications that list agencies, services, and resources for blind and visually impaired persons.

"Corporate Resources Available to Assist Individuals with Disabilities." *Illinois Libraries: Library Services for Persons with Handicaps,* Vol. 72, No. 4, April, 1990, pp. 375-78.

*Directory of National Organizations and Centers of and for Deaf and Hard of Hearing People.* Galludet University, Washington, DC, National Information Center on Deafness, 800 Florida Ave., NE, Washington, DC 20002.

*Directory of Services for Blind and Visually Impaired Persons in the United States.* New York: American Federation for the Blind, 1989.

A comprehensive guide and information source on organizations, service providers, vendors of equipment, and service sites around the nation.

*Disability Rights Guide: Practical Solutions to Problems Affecting People with Disabilities.* Charles D. Goldman, Esq., Lincoln, NE: Media Publishing, 1987.

Although this book does not cover the ADA, it is still valuable, especially for the state-by-state guide to laws and contacts.

*1990 Resource Guide to Organizations Concerned with Developmental Handicaps.* American Association of University Affiliated Programs for Persons with Developmental Disabilities. Request from the National Maternal and Child Health Clearinghouse, 38th and R St., NW, Washington, DC 20057, (202) 625-8410. Or, order for $3.00 from the National Health Information Center, P.O. Box 1133, Washington, DC 20013-1133, (800) 336-4797.

*Support Organizations.* IBM National Support Center for Persons with Disabilities. Voice: (800) 426-2133; TDD: (800) 284-9482, P.O. Box 2150, Atlanta, GA 30301-2150. Free. 64 pages.

Lists local, state, and regional organizations and describes the services provided.

*Technology for Persons with Disabilities—An Introduction.* Voice: (800) 426-2133; TDD: (800) 284-9482; P.O. Box 2150, Atlanta, GA 30301-2150. Free. 54 pages.

Lists national support groups, service providers, and publishers of relevant periodicals. Indexed.

*USA Quick Guide for the Deaf Community.* Part 1 is published by the District of Columbia Public Library, Washington, DC. Part 2 is published by the National Association of the Deaf and is available for $5.00 from NAD/FOLDA-USA, 814 Thayer Ave., Silver Spring, MD 20910.

Some states also have guides available from their state association for the deaf.

*See also* the resource list entitled "Library Services for People with Disabilities" earlier in this chapter. Many of the publications given there list organizations.

# AUXILIARY AIDS

## Organizations

**Alliance for Technology Access (ATA),** 1307 Solano Ave., Albany, CA 94706-1888, Voice: (415) 528-0747.
Provides helpful information on micro-computer technology for children and adults with disabilities.

**American Foundation for the Blind (AFB),** National Technology Center, 15 West 16th St., New York, NY 10011, Voice: (800) 232-5463.
Supplies information on visual impairment and blindness, technology, and products and publications.

**Apple Computer, Inc.,** Office of Special Education & Rehabilitation, 26525 Mariani Ave., M/435, Cupertino, CA 95014, Voice: (408) 974-7910; TDD: (408) 7911.

**AT&T National Special Needs Center,** 2001 Route 46, Suite 310, Parsippany, NJ 07054-9990, Voice: (800) 233-1222; TDD: (800) 833-3232.

**Center for Special Education Technology,** The Council for Exceptional Children, 1920 Association Dr., Reston, VA 22091-1589, Voice: (800) 873-8255.
Distributes information on assistive-technology. Also operates a monthly bulletin board on SPECIALNET; (800) 345-TECH for taped messages on technology.

**Electronic Industries Foundation (EIF),** The Rehabilitation Engineer Center (REC), 1901 Pennsylvania Ave., NW, Suite 700, Washington, DC 20006, Voice: (202) 955-5810.
Provides general information on assistive devices and their applications.

**IBM National Support Center for Persons with Disabilities,** P.O. Box 2150, Atlanta, GA 30301-2150, Voice: (800) 426-2133; TDD: (800) 284-9482.
Provides products, information, and services. Free publications include Technology for Persons with Disabilities—An Introduction; Resource Guide for Persons with Mobility Impairments; Resource Guide for Persons with Learning Impairments; IBM Personal System/2 SpeechViewer; Resource Guide for Persons with Hearing Impairments; Resource Guide for Persons with Speech or Language Impairments; and Resource Guide for Persons with Vision Impairments.

**National Information Center on Deafness,** Gallaudet University, 800 Florida Ave., NE, Washington, DC 20002, Voice: (202) 651-5051.
Publishes brief resource listings and descriptive fact sheets on requested topics for a nominal fee.

**National Rehabilitation Information Center**, 8455 Coilesville Road, Suite 935, Silver Spring, MD 20910.

Maintains a clearinghouse on available services and equipment.

**S.M.A.R.T. Exchange,** P.O. Box 724704, Atlanta, GA 30339.

This regional information exchange funded by the National Institute on Disability and Rehabilitation Research provides free publications, resource guides, and reference tools on new equipment.

**Trace Center, University of Wisconsin,** Waisman Center, 1500 Highland Ave., Madison, WI 53705, Voice: (608) 262-6966.

Provides information related to nonvocal communication, computer access, and technology.

## Publications

*Assistive Technology Sourcebook,* Alexandra Enders and Marian Hall, eds. Washington, DC: Resna Press, 1990.

This comprehensive tool for finding out about assistive technology contains explanations of assistive items, methods of finding them, and some evaluative information. It should be available for public reference and can also be of use to the library service provider.

*Extend Their Reach,* Electronic Industries Association, Consumer Electronics Group, 2001 Pennsylvania Ave., NW, Washington DC 2006-1813, (202) 457-4919. Pamphlet. 24 pages. $.65 each.

Introduces the types of products available to overcome impairment of sight, speech, hearing, and motion. Describes how the member companies of ADD (the Assistive Devices Division) of the EIA network create and sell assistive devices of every kind.

*The First Whole Rehab Catalog: A Comprehensive Guide to Products and Services for the Physically Disadvantaged,* A. Jay Abrams & Margaret Ann Abrams. White Hall, Virginia: Bitterway Publications, 1990.

Provides comprehensive listing, description, and ordering information on products for a variety of disability needs. Includes a resource list and addresses of technology information centers, federal agencies, and advocacy groups.

*Illinois Libraries: Library Services for Persons with Handicaps,* Vol. 72, No. 4, April, 1990, pp. 378-89. Back issues free.

*The Illustrated Directory of Handicap Products,* Trio Publications, 3600 W. Timber Ct., Lawrence, KS 66049, (913) 749-1453. $12.95 and $2.50 postage.

*Library Outreach Reporter,* 1671 East 16th St., Suite 226, Brooklyn, NY 11229, Voice: (718) 645-2396.

Provides an annual selected list of products and aids catalogs.

*Resource Inventory: State Grants P.L. 100-407,* Center for Special Education Technology, 1920 Association Dr., Reston, VA 22091-1589, (800) 873-8255. This is a list of agencies providing information and services under the Technology-Related Assistance for Individuals with Disabilities Act of 1988.

*Resources for People with Disabilities and Chronic Conditions,* 1991. Available from Resources for Rehabilitation, 33 Bedford St., Lexington, MA 02173. $44.95.

## Computerized Databases

**ABLEDATA,** The National Rehabilitation Information Center (NARIC), 4407 8th St., NE, Washington, DC 20017, Voice: (202) 635-5826.

Provides reliable and extensive listings of available products designed to service people with disabilities. Manufacturer, availability information, price, description, and comments regarding devices useful to persons with disabilities are included.

**Accent on Information,** P.O. Box 700, Bloomington, IL 61701.

**Assistive Device Database System Assistive Device Resource Center,** California State University, 6000 J St., Sacramento, CA 95819, Voice: (916) 454-6422.

Provides over 6,000 informational items related to aids and devices, disability service organizations, helpful publications, and innovations for computer use. The *Buyer's Guide* is published annually. Information on assistive devices is published with a wide range of resource listings. Focus is given to educational needs of people with disabilities, and a bibliography is included.

**CTG (Closing the Gap) Solutions,** Closing the Gap, P.O. Box 68, Henderson, MN 56044, Voice: (612) 248-3294.

An information retrieval system that is focused on products and use of computer services relative to disabilities.

**National Technology Database,** American Foundation for the Blind, National Technology Center, 15 West 16th St., New York, NY 10011, Voice: (212) 620-2080.

Provides information on products for the blind.

# EMPLOYMENT—RESOURCES

## Organizations

**Job Accommodation Network (JAN),** West Virginia University, 809 Allen Hall, P.O. Box 6123, Morgantown, WV 26506-6122, Voice: (304) 293-7186; Voice/TDD: (800) 526-7234; Inside West Virginia, Voice/TDD: (800) 526-4698; Canada, Voice/TDD: (800) 526-2262.

JAN is an international information network and consulting resource for enabling qualified workers with disabilities to be hired or retained. It brings together information from many sources about practical ways of making accommodations for employees and applicants with disabilities. JAN offers comprehensive information on methods and available equipment that have proven effective for a wide range of accommodations. These accommodations are usually not expensive. JAN is a service of the President's Committee on Employment of People with Disabilities.

**Mainstream, Inc.,** 1030 15th St., NW, Suite 1010, Washington, DC 20005, Voice/TDD: (202) 898-0202.

Mainstream helps individuals with disabilities move into the workplace; it publishes numerous useful guides for employers on hiring, accommodating, and supervising individuals with specific disabilities. Mainstream offers an *ADA Management Kit* for $39.95 to help employers (order from Mainstream, P.O. Box 65183, Washington, DC 20005-5183).

## Publications

*Fighting for the Rights of Disabled Employees: An AFSCME Guide.* Originally developed in 1984 by the American Federation of State, County and Municipal Employees, updated in 1990. Available free to AFSCME members from AFSCME International Research Department, 1625 L St., Washington, DC 20036, (202) 429-1215.

This guide provides information on how to handle many of the problems that workers with disabilities face and outlines a variety of strategies for assisting such workers.

*Library Resources on the Employment of Individuals with Disabilities.* U.S. Equal Employment Opportunity Commission Library, November, 1990. Available from EEOC, 1801 L St., NW, Washington, DC 20507, (202) 663-4630.

This is an annotated bibliography of print and audiovisual resources on the employment of people with disabilities that are available in the EEOC Library. Materials listed can be requested through interlibrary loan.

*Part of the Team: People with Disabilities in the Workforce.* Video, 30 min. Available in VHS and 3/4 inch and open captioned, 1990. Order from National

Easter Seal Society, Communications Department, 70 East Lake St., Chicago, IL 60601. Voice: (312) 726-6200; TDD: (312) 726-4258; $15, VHS; $25, 3/4".
Produced by the President's Committee on Employment of People with Disabilities, IBM, and the National Easter Seal Society. Available in all U.S. Equal Employment Opportunity Commission field offices. This video presents stories of 10 employed persons with disabilities and how their needs are accommodated by employers. The stories will help employers prepare to accommodate and work with disabilities.

*Reading, Willing, and Available: A Business Guide for Hiring People with Disabilities.* Free from the President's Committee on Employment of People with Disabilities, 1111 20th St., NW, Suite 636, Washington, DC 20036-3470. Voice: (202) 653-5044; TDD: (202) 653-5050.
This publication contains a job analysis form to assist employers in analyzing physical requirements of a job and other useful tips. Also available from the President's Committee are two pamphlets: *Employer Guide: Simple Steps to Job Accommodation* and *Employer Guide: How to Successfully Supervise Employees with Disabilities.*

*The Workplace Workbook: An Illustrated Guide to Job Accommodations and Assistive Technology,* James Mueller. Dole Foundation, 1990. Available from The Dole Foundation, 1819 H St., NW, Suite 850, Washington, DC 20005-3603. Voice/TDD: (202) 457-0318.

## CHAPTER 3
# The Impact of the ADA upon School Library Media Centers

Prior to the passage of the Americans with Disabilities Act of 1990 (ADA), a number of laws aimed at ensuring access to educational facilities and services were passed by the United States Congress. Educational systems in this country have been significantly affected by this body of legislation, beginning as early as 1965. School library media centers, like all components of school systems, have already made important changes in facilities and services in order to implement these laws. We know, however, that civil rights laws are not always as effective as intended. Certainly, one of the most sweeping of the laws affecting school children with disabilities, Public Law 94-142, the Education for all Handicapped Children Act of 1975, has not worked nearly as well as envisioned.[1] If previous laws have been widely and effectively implemented, the ADA should have little direct impact upon school library media centers. There may, however, be indirect effects from the ADA upon school library media centers, and media specialists should take advantage of the opportunities and possibilities which the law offers.

## HISTORY OF LEGISLATION AFFECTING THE EDUCATION OF CHILDREN WITH DISABILITIES

In order to understand why most provisions of the ADA should already have been implemented in school library media centers, it is necessary to understand the historical development of educational and civil rights for children with disabilities and the previous legislation which guaranteed these rights. Adult caregivers for the children, particularly parents and guardians, but in many cases even educators, do not always understand the extent of these rights. The National Information Center for Children and Youth with Disabilities, or NICHCY (the retained acronym of the agency's former name, the National Information Center for Handicapped Children and Youth), reported that even though there has been since the 1960s "a virtual avalanche of Federal legislation that relates directly or indirectly to individuals with disabilities, particularly children and youth . . . many families and professionals have little knowledge about the laws."[2] According to NICHCY, a 1989 survey conducted by Louis Harris and Associates for the International Center for the Disabled found that

> 61% of the parents surveyed knew little or nothing about their rights under both the Education of the Handicapped Act (EHA) Public Law 94-142 and Section 504 of the Rehabilitation Act of 1973—Public Law 93-112. Even a greater number of these parents—85%—were not aware of the vocational education law, the Carl D. Perkins Vocational Education Act of 1984—Public Law 98-524. Finally, a majority of both principals and teachers surveyed felt they had not had adequate training in special education.[3]

Since the three laws mentioned in this passage, along with the ADA, are landmark legislation affecting education for children and youth with disabilities, it is imperative that both parents and educators understand their rights and responsibilities under these laws. Therefore, this chapter will discuss at length the provisions of these and other laws which affect schools as a whole, as well as school library media centers.

In the early years of our country, people with disabilities were hidden away at home or confined to institutions; no education or training was provided. In the nineteenth century, various states began to establish residential schools and asylums for children who were blind, deaf, or mentally retarded. The first federal law regarding children with disabilities was Public Law 19-8, the Education of the Handicapped, which in 1828 "provided assistance to establish a school for the deaf in Kentucky."[4] The education in such institutions was still very limited; children with disabilities were not expected to become functioning members of society. By the beginning of the twentieth century, day programs of special education were being established in public schools, and during the second decade of this century, New

Jersey, New York, and Massachusetts were pioneers among the states in enacting legislation requiring education of children with disabilities.[5] Special education programs were relatively common by mid-century. Nevertheless, Velleman (1964) reported that in 1958 only one-fourth of the children with disabilities between ages 5 and 17 were receiving an appropriate education; 83% of these were educated at the elementary level. She found that "the orthopedically disabled and those with special health problems" were the least likely to be appropriately educated.[6] From my own experience, I would add that children who were more than mildly retarded were often not receiving an education at that time.

Much of the advancement made in education for children with disabilities since 1960 had been due to the work of the so-called consumer movement, led by organizations for parents of children with disabilities, adults with disabilities, and other advocates.[7] The civil rights movement became the prototype for those who sought similar rights for people with disabilities:

> It was *Brown v. Board of Education*[8] that most forcefully stated the philosophy of integration. That decision was based on the federal constitutional principle of the Fourteenth Amendment, which provides that the states may not deprive anyone of "life, liberty, or property, without due process of law" nor deny anyone "equal protection of the laws."[9] While it has been consistently held by the [U. S.] Supreme Court that there is no federally protected right to education, nonetheless if the state undertakes to provide education (which all states do), a property interest is thereby created by the state. The *Brown* decision recognized that educating Black children separately, even if done so in "equal" facilities, was inherently unequal because of the stigma attached to being educated separately and because of the deprivation of interaction with children of other backgrounds.[10]

Many people soon began to deplore the separate education of children with disabilities. However, the landmark Civil Rights Act of 1964, which barred discrimination in employment and public accommodations based on race, sex, religion, or national origin, did not include people with disabilities. Similar rights for them were fully guaranteed only with the passage of the ADA.

Federal support for the education of children with disabilities began with Public Law 89-10, the Elementary and Secondary Education Act of 1965 (ESEA), which sought to strengthen and improve educational quality and opportunity in the nation's schools. Title V authorized grants to state departments of education to provide assistance and service to local education agencies. Among the "aspects of education" to be addressed was "services to the handicapped."[11] Title II provided grants "for the acquisition of school library resources, textbooks, and other printed and published instructional materials."[12] Between 1966 and 1982, the federal government distributed $1,944,928,275 to the states for library and instructional materials under Title II and, later, under Title IV-B.[13] In addition, school library media specialists were often able to utilize funds, distributed under the ESEA for other programs such as the Title I programs, to buy materials which could be placed in the library media center for the use of the students in the relevant program.

Eight months after the passage of the ESEA, Public Law 89-313, the Elementary and Secondary Education Act Amendments of 1965, authorized grants to state agencies for the education of children with disabilities in state-operated or state-supported schools and institutions. This was the first federal grant program for children and youth with disabilities. The next year, grants for the education of children and youth with disabilities were authorized at the local level by Title VI of Public Law 89-750, the Elementary and Secondary Education Act Amendments of 1966. This law also established the Bureau of Education for the Handicapped (BEH) to administer all programs for such students in the U.S. Office of Education.

> BEH was charged with helping states to: implement and monitor programs; support demonstration programs; conduct research and evaluate federally funded programs; provide financial support for training special educators, other teachers, support personnel, and parents; and to support research, training, production, and distribution of educational media.[14]

Finally, Public Law 89-750 established the National Advisory Council, now called the National Council on Disability. This body "is charged with reviewing all laws, programs, and policies of the Federal Government affecting individuals with disabilities, and making such recommendations as it deems necessary to the President, the Congress, the Secretary of the Department of Education, the Commissioner of the Rehabilitation Services Administration, and the Director of the National Institute of Disability and Rehabilitation Research."[15]

Public Law 90-247, the Elementary and Secondary Education Act Amendments of 1968, provided for a wide range of discretionary programs for special education:

. . .funding for regional resource centers, centers and services for children with deaf-blindness, the expansion of instructional media programs, continued research in special education, and funds to establish a center to help improve the recruitment of education personnel and to disseminate information concerning educational opportunities for children and youth with disabilities.[16]

These amendments supported both services of school library media programs and of special education.

Public Law 91-230, the Elementary and Secondary Education Act Amendments of 1970, consolidated a number of federal grant programs for the education of children with disabilities in Part B, which became known as the Education of the Handicapped Act (EHA). It was the forerunner of the Education for All Handicapped Children Act. Four years later, Public Law 93-380, the Education for All Handicapped Act Amendments of 1974

required states to establish a time-table toward achieving full educational opportunity for all children with disabilities. The Act provided procedural safeguards for use in the identification, evaluation, and placement of children with disabilities, mandated that such children be integrated into regular classes when possible, and required assurances that testing and evaluation materials be selected and administered on a nondiscriminatory basis . . . . [This law] was important because it began the focus . . . on fully educating all children with disabilities.[17]

Meanwhile, organizations and citizens interested in the education of children with disabilities were taking their case to the state legislatures and courts. In 1972, two cases involving the education of children with disabilities resulted in landmark legal decisions which established important precedents for future laws. *Pennsylvania Association for Retarded Children (PARC) vs. Pennsylvania* was a class action suit brought by PARC on behalf of 13 children with mental retardation. PARC argued that the fourteenth amendment to the United States Constitution guarantees due process and equal protection under the laws; therefore, these children were entitled to the same access to education that other children enjoyed. The case ended in a consent agreement which stipulated that children with mental retardation were capable of benefiting from education and were entitled to a free, public education appropriate to their capacity. The state was required to identify all school-aged children with mental retardation who were not in school and to place them in a suitable program. The most desirable situation was to place the children in a regular school whenever possible.

The second landmark case, *Mills vs. Board of Education*, was also argued under the equal protection and due process clauses of the U. S. Constitution. Parents of seven children with disabilities brought a class action suit against the school board of the District of Columbia on behalf of all children with disabilities. The case resulted in a judgment against the school board. The court ordered that all children, regardless of their disability or its severity, were entitled to a public education. To the argument that this would result in an undue economic burden, the court stated that if this were true, "the available funds must be expended equitably in such a manner that no child is entirely excluded from a publicly supported education."[18] By 1976, over 40 similar cases had been brought; in all cases the decision upheld the right of children with disabilities to a public education.[19] Also by 1976, all states except Mississippi and Ohio had passed legislation mandating education for children with disabilities.

The first of the landmark laws mentioned above, and the first major federal law ensuring the civil rights of people with disabilities was Public Law 93-112, the Rehabilitation Act of 1973. It was wide-ranging, but it is Section 504, Non-Discrimination under Federal Grants, which is of particular importance to schools and libraries. It stated that a person with disabilities could not "solely by reason of his [or her] handicap, be excluded from the participation in, be denied the benefits of, or be subjected to discrimination under any program or activity receiving Federal financial assistance."[20] To receive the benefits of this law, however, the person in question must meet the definition of a disabled person:

> any person who (i) has a physical or mental impairment which substantially limits one or more of such person's major life activities, (ii) has a record of such an impairment, or (iii) is regarded as having such an impairment.[21]

"Major life activities" were defined as caring for one's self, performing manual tasks, walking, seeing, hearing, speaking, breathing, learning, and working.[22] This law was of the utmost importance to schools and libraries, since most of them receive some form of federal aid. Rather than lose federal funds, most such institutions sought to bring their programs into compliance with the law.

With Section 504 of the Rehabilitation Act of 1973, many people think first of structural modifications which allow people with mobility impairments to access the building, but the law was aimed at program accessibility. Structural modifications are not necessary if the program can be effectively taken to an individual with disabilities, although using the same setting as that for service to nondisabled people is preferable.[23] Nevertheless, after the passage of this bill, many schools and libraries began to make structural changes which increased building access. It was fairly easy to assign children with disabilities to accessible classrooms (if necessary the entire class could be relocated), but there was only one media center per school. Therefore, school library media centers, like cafeterias, auditoriums, and restrooms, were often primary targets for renovation.

The second landmark law was, of course, Public Law 94-142, the Education for All Handicapped Children Act of 1975, which went into effect in 1977. (Like Public Laws 91-230 and 93-380, this law is often known as the EHA, but EAHCA will be used here to refer specifically to it.) The law was the result of a decade of other laws, court decisions, and advocacy by and for people with disabilities. Its purpose was

> to assure that all handicapped children have available to them . . . a free appropriate public education which emphasizes special education and related services designed to meet their unique needs, to assure that the rights of handicapped children and their parents or guardians are protected, to assist states and localities to provide for the education of all handicapped children, and to assess and assure the effectiveness of efforts to educate handicapped children.[24]

Among the services required by the law were nondiscriminatory and multi-disciplinary assessment of educational needs, parental involvement in the development of the child's educational program, education in the least restrictive environment, and an Individualized Educational Program, or IEP.[25] Parents have the right to challenge and appeal decisions if they do not concur with their child's placement. One point is important for school library media specialists: the law states that children who need them are entitled to related services, including such things as speech pathology, audiology, psychological services, physical and occupational therapy, recreation, and counseling. It does not mention library media services. However, "the list of related services is not exhaustive and may include other developmental, corrective, or supportive services (such as artistic and cultural programs, and art, music, and dance therapy), if they are required to assist a handicapped child to benefit from special education."[26] If children need special help in using the school library media center and its materials, this could be made a part of the IEP.

Under the EAHCA, the federal government provides partial funding for children with disabilities. Unlike most federal grant laws, it does not have an expiration date.[27] States are not required to take advantage of Public Law 94-142 unless they wish to receive federal funding, but all states do so, probably because they are required to provide many of the same services under Section 504. This law, however, cannot compare with the EAHCA, since it is much less extensive and does not include the funding incentive. It is unnecessary to say much more about Public Law 94-142; the literature about it is substantial. (For example, see National Council on Disability, 1989; National Information Center for Children and Youth with Disabilities, 1991; and Rothstein, 1990, in the references at the end of this chapter.)

Public Law 98-199, the Education of the Handicapped Act Amendments of 1983, expanded incentives for preschool special education programs, early intervention, and transition programs (from school to work). It also placed all EHA programs under the U.S. Office of Special Education Programs (OSEP), which superseded BEH. Children ages 3 to 21 were covered under Public Law 94-142, but Public Law 99-457, the Education of the Handicapped Act Amendments of 1986, greatly expanded services to preschool children. Additional funding for special education and related services for children aged 3 to 5 was included, and an early intervention plan for children with disabilities aged birth through two years was instituted. The plan called for "a statewide, comprehensive, coordinated, multidisciplinary interagency program" for those infants and toddlers who "need early intervention services because of developmental delays or who have a diagnosed physical or mental condition that has a high probability of resulting in developmental delay."[28] An Individualized Family Services Plan (IFSP) must be developed for infant or toddler and their family. Unlike services for children aged 3 to 5, the program for infants and toddlers was not necessarily administered by the state education agency; any state agency could be eligible to do so by meeting the requirements of the law. Also in 1986, Public Law 99-372, the Handicapped Children's Protection Act, authorized the award of attorneys' fees and costs to parents or guardians who are the prevailing parties in due process and judicial proceedings under the EAHCA.

Meanwhile, Public Law 98-524, the Vocational Education Act of 1984, often called the Carl D. Perkins Act, was the third of the landmark laws to be passed. This Act aims to improve access to vocational education for those who have been underserved in the past or who have greater than average educational needs. Students with disabilities are specifically included. Such students are entitled to equal access to recruitment, enrollment, and placement activities, and to a full range of vocational education programs. Vocational education planning should be coordinated between vocational education, special education, and vocational rehabilitation agencies, and it should be consistent with the student's IEP.[29]

Many people with disabilities can benefit greatly from adaptive and assistive technological devices. Public Law 100-407, the Technology-Related Assistance for Individuals with Disabilities Act of 1988, addressed this issue. Despite its name, it does not provide direct technological support to individuals. Title I provides funds for states to use in developing a consumer-responsive state system of assistive technology services. States may do this through such means as model delivery systems, state-wide needs assessments, support groups, public awareness programs, training and technical assistance, access to related information, and interagency agreements. Title II authorizes federal activities to help states develop delivery systems.

An amendment to this Act, Public Law 101-392, the Carl D. Perkins Vocational and Applied Technology Education Act of 1990, also recognized the need for technological assistance. It "will concentrate resources on improving educational programs leading to the academic and occupational skill competencies needed to work in a technologically advanced society."[30] It is closely interwoven with another 1990 law, Public Law 101-476, the Education of the Handicapped Act Amendments of 1990. This law changed the name of the Education of the Handicapped Act (EHA) to Individuals with Disabilities Education Act (IDEA). It expanded many programs and added new ones. It also included transition programs and technology services as special education services which must be included in a child's IEP.

This rather extensive discussion of laws which preceded the ADA shows that most of its provisions were already mandated for schools, and therefore for school library media centers. We shall now seek to discover ways in which media centers will be affected by the ADA.

## DIRECT EFFECTS OF THE ADA

As noted earlier, the ADA will have relatively little direct impact upon school library media centers because almost all aspects of the ADA are already in effect there. Titles IV and V of the ADA, which deal with Telecommunications and Miscellaneous Provisions, as well as Subtitle B of Title II, dealing with Public Transportation, do not affect school library media centers. Title I (Employment) extends to all employers the same types of regulations which have long been in force in schools under Section 504 of the Rehabilitation Act of 1973. That law requires nondiscrimination in employment in all entities which receive any federal funding. That immediately included almost all schools, whether public, private, or parochial. Under the ESEA, federal funds were made available to private as well as public schools for services, such as school library resources, textbooks, and other instructional materials. Very few schools and school systems could afford to turn down these funds. Therefore, only a few schools not already covered under Section 504 will be included under the ADA.

Title II of the ADA provides that "no qualified individual with a disability shall . . . be excluded from participation in or be denied the benefits of the services, programs, or activities of a public entity."[31] Section 504 already mandates program accessibility of entities receiving federal funds; Public Law 94-142 assures access to school services for children with disabilities. Most public schools are thus already covered. We can assume that these laws already mandate the rights of physical accessibility to the school library media center for children with disabilities and to materials in formats appropriate for their use. The National Council on Disabilities (1989) has shown that even under Public Law 94-142, children with disabilities do not always receive an appropriate education. It is doubtful that the ADA will change that. If the lure of funding, which is present under Public Law 94-142, will not suffice to secure equal rights, the more negative motivation of the ADA is unlikely to do so.

There is one area where Title II may have some impact. The U.S. Department of Justice regulations (28 *CFR* Part 35) address situations in which parents and other people with disabilities, who are not covered by the Individuals with Disabilities Act, wish to attend programs open to parents or the public. "Graduation ceremonies, parent-teacher organization meetings, plays and other events open to the public, and adult education classes,"[32] are specifically mentioned. Access to such activities must be provided; appropriate auxiliary aids and services must also be provided. Clearly, a situation of this kind might arise in a school library media center. Parent-teacher organization meetings often are held in media centers; parents must be able to attend. Even if meetings are not held in the media center, parents should be able to visit it to examine materials provided for their children and to use materials provided for parents. A parent who is deaf may need an interpreter when attending meetings or when talking with the media specialist about selecting materials for her or his child. A TDD (Telecommunication Devices for the Deaf) might be needed when the parent or the media specialist want to contact each other. A person with visual impairment might require enlargement of materials; a blind parent might need access to materials in Braille. Although the cost of providing a closed-circuit television system (CCTV) to enlarge materials or a computer which translates to and from Braille might be an undue burden upon the school, it is clear that the school library media specialist must make some accommodation for parents and other people with disabilities. Parent notices and newsletters might be provided in large print. (Large scale fonts for a computer are not prohibitively expensive and can be used for many other purposes.) If a person cannot reach high shelves, someone must take the books down for him or her, and if he or she cannot see or hold the book, someone must read it to him or her. If books on parenting or professional books for teachers are provided, the library must be prepared to provide such materials in large print, Braille, or audiotape, if needed. Similar accommodations will be needed in other situations.

"Goods, services, facilities, privileges, advantages, and accommodations" must be provided in "the most integrated setting appropriate to the needs of the individual."[33] Special services may be provided for people with disabilities, but the people concerned may choose to participate in the activities provided for the general public and refuse to participate in the special services. Thus the school must be prepared to offer parents and other community members who participate in school activities the same services offered everyone. In the library media center, in addition to the items mentioned above, this may include providing accessible facilities and materials for adult education students who are disabled.

Under Title II, public entities must provide program accessibility unless it causes an undue burden. Given the financial problems in many school libraries today, providing auxiliary aids and devices and books in special formats for parents and other adults may seem an undue burden. One solution might be a district-wide collection of National Library Service for the Blind and Physically Handicapped (NLS) materials in special formats which could be loaned to schools that have parents or adult education students with particular disabilities in their service area. There is another possibility, if there are enough people with disabilities in the school's service area; a deposit collection of materials in suitable format, such as talking books and equipment, and in Braille is available from the state's NLS regional network library for the blind and physically handicapped (or subregional talking book library in your area if there is one).

Title III of the ADA applies to Public Accommodations and Services Operated by Private Entities. Among those specifically mentioned in the law are "a museum, library, gallery, or other place of public display or collection," and "a nursery, elementary, secondary, undergraduate, or postgraduate private school, or other place of education."[34] Thus most private schools which are not already subject to the provisions of Section 504 of the Rehabilitation Act of 1973 will have to meet the requirements of the ADA. The U. S. Department of Justice regulations make clear that private schools are covered by the ADA as places of public accommodation, but that "the rule . . . does not require a private school to provide a free appropriate education or develop an individualized education program."[35] However, the receipt of federal assistance by the school would require compliance with these laws "to the extent mandated by the particular type of assistance received." Religious organizations, including schools operated by a religious body, are exempt from the requirements of the ADA, even if their services are open to the general public. Schools controlled by religious organizations are also exempt, even if the organization uses a lay board to operate them. Again, however, such schools are subject to Section 504 of the Rehabilitation Act of 1973 if they receive federal funds.

Although they apply to different entities, Title II and Title III are very similar in their applications. However, the law is less stringent in regard to private entities than toward public ones. Public entities have to provide accessibility unless it is an "undue burden"; public accommodations and services operated by private entities must provide accessibility if it is "readily achievable." This is defined as being "easily accomplishable and able to be carried out without much difficulty and expense."[36] Decisions on what is readily achievable and what is not must be decided on a case-by-case basis. Building a ramp for wheelchair access might be considered readily achievable; putting in an elevator might not. In the example used above, that of a parent who is disabled, library media centers which fall under Title III do not have to stock "accessible or special goods . . . such as Brailled versions of books, books on audio-cassettes, [and] closed-captioned video tapes"[37] but must be prepared to order them upon request if the library regularly orders such materials. This, of course, could be done through interlibrary loan. Entities are expected to make reasonable modifications in policies, practices, and procedures when such modifications are necessary, unless the modifications would fundamentally alter the nature of its services. Changes in circulation and reserve policies for people with disabilities, who may not be able to get to the school or media center easily or who may need extra time to use materials, would be considered reasonable. Telephone renewal, extended circulation periods, and allowing home use of reserve materials are examples of such policy changes. School library media specialists should be willing to make special provisions, based on the needs of individual students, to allow maximum use of their materials.

## INDIRECT EFFECTS OF THE ADA

Although the ADA will have relatively little direct impact upon school library media centers, the indirect impact may be more extensive. Probably its chief effect will be to make school personnel, parents, and students more aware of the rights to which people with disabilities are entitled. Although most school library media centers are already providing accessible programs and equal employment opportunities, the ADA will initiate a new period of awareness of the issue among the general public as well as the school community. Media attention will be turned to the implementation of the ADA, and many people who have not thought recently about the rights of people with disabilities will do so. School library media specialists will have a fine opportunity to assess their program and improve it at this time.

It can be expected that the future will see more individuals with disabilities seeking employment. Many children with disabilities have now received the benefits of Public Law 94-142 during their entire elementary and secondary education. "As a direct result of this statute . . . students with disabilities . . . began knocking on the doors of colleges and universities around the country, saying, 'I am that "otherwise handicapped individual" that Section 504 says you are to serve.'"[38] Many of those students, however, discovered when they graduated from college that however qualified they were, they could not find jobs. Students with less education found the job search even harder. Many people with disabilities did not try to find work; they were conditioned by past experiences and expectations to see themselves as unable to participate in employment. Many employers were not required to hire persons with disabilities. As the ADA goes into effect, most employers will be unable to refuse employment to an otherwise qualified applicant because of a disability. Furthermore, accessible public transportation, mandated by Title II, Part B of the

ADA, may make it possible for some people with disabilities who previously could not get to work to do so.

This situation will probably have two effects on schools and therefore on school library media centers. First, in the future, there may well be more school employees with disabilities. Although Section 504 of the Rehabilitation Act of 1973 already requires that programs that receive federal funds, which includes most schools, cannot discriminate in employment, the ADA and the awareness it encourages may cause more people with disabilities to seek employment in schools. A school library media specialist may find that he or she is serving more teachers with disabilities. He or she may find that more people applying for jobs as library aides and paraprofessionals are disabled. In fact, the school library media specialist may have a disability. He or she will need to learn how to structure the job to accommodate an employee who is disabled. A library media center employee with a disability can serve as a positive role model for students with disabilities, encouraging them to enter the library media field.

Secondly, the ADA, along with existing laws like IDEA and the Carl D. Perkins Vocational Act, will encourage more students to stay in school, to seek vocational training, and to enter postsecondary education. It has been suggested that the Individualized Educational Program or IEP should include recommendations "not only for vocational preparation, but also to vocational awareness and vocational exploration."[39] School library media centers usually assist students and vocational teachers and counselors by providing materials about various vocations and their requirements, college and university catalogs and admission requirements, and other pertinent information which helps students in the transition to work or higher education. Parents and advocates for students with disabilities often want such materials also. Media centers will need to provide more information of this nature for students who have disabilities. Reference books, periodicals, catalogs, vertical file materials computer programs, and audiovisual materials will all be needed to provide suitable materials in accessible formats.

Another important indirect effect of the ADA will be an increased number of self-evaluations by affected programs. Under the U.S. Department of Justice regulations all public entities are required to do a self-evaluation of their current policies and practices to identify and correct those that are inconsistent with the Act. Entities which have already done such a self-evaluation under Section 504 of the Rehabilitation Act of 1973 do not have to do another, except for policies and practices, such as communication access, which were not previously required. The U.S. Department of Justice notes that "most self-evaluations were done five to twelve years ago, however, [and] the Department expects that a great many public entities will be reexamining all of their policies and programs."[40] Individuals with disabilities or organizations representing them must be given an opportunity to participate in the evaluations. Self-evaluations will probably be carried out at the district and school levels, but a school library media specialist should take the time to make a self-examination of his or her own program. Is it in full compliance with the many laws which affect the education of students with disabilities? Are there areas in which he or she could help other educators serve the children? Does he or she have a positive attitude toward people with disabilities, an awareness of their problems, and a knowledge of how the disability affects the individual? The matter of attitude is particularly important; Jane Jarrow said that "attitudinal barriers . . . [are], perhaps, more important than physical accessibility to true integration of students with disabilities."[41]

## OPPORTUNITIES AND POSSIBILITIES OFFERED BY THE ADA

In addition to direct and indirect effects of the ADA, the law opens some opportunities and possibilities to school library media specialists and their programs. These opportunities and possibilities will be presented here within the context of *Information Power*, the current guidelines for school library media programs. *Information Power* outlines three roles for school library media specialists: information specialist, teacher, and instructional consultant. The ADA offers opportunities and possibilities which are connected with each of these roles.

One aspect of the role of information specialist, providing expanded information about employment, vocational training, and postsecondary education for students with disabilities, was discussed above. As the ADA builds public awareness of people with disabilities, information on their rights and needs will be desired by many people, including educators, parents, advocates, and students. If school library media specialists collect and disseminate information to meet this need, they will contribute to the public's awareness of their own program at the same time that they contribute to its awareness of disabling conditions and disability rights. They do not have to wait for others to ask for information. They themselves can call attention to the ADA through such means as newsletters to the school community, bulletin boards, and displays. They can recommend materials from the library media center collection which deal with the ADA and people with disabilities. They can build a file of information on local organizations and accessible facilities, and act as a referral agency. They can make self-evaluations and issue reports on the accessibility of the media center program.

One of the elements which *Information Power* mentions in regard to this role is that of developing flexible policies for use of resources. This is especially important for students with disabilities, who often need extra time to read or complete assignments. The students may require materials in audiovisual formats, which often take longer to view or hear than it would take to read the same material. Other students with disabilities may have communication problems, including poor reading skills, which slow them down. Still others may have mobility problems that prevent them from getting to the library media center in time to check out materials in high demand. Flexible circulation and reserve policies may be needed to accommodate students with disabilities.

In the teaching role, school library media specialists have the obligation, as well as the opportunity, to teach information literacy skills to students with disabilities. Another teaching opportunity is the development of positive attitudes toward people with disabilities. Workshops to promote this can be conducted by library media specialists for students, teachers, and parents. A library media specialist or media center staff member who has a disability can demonstrate the capabilities of people with disabilities through their own example. Student assistants should not be forgotten. A disability does not disqualify a child or young adult for this position. They, too, can serve as role models and can alter other people's perceptions of those with disabilities.

Service to students with disabilities fits naturally into the library media specialist's third role, information consultant. Library media specialists routinely use their knowledge of resources, media, and technologies to help teachers and students select the best materials for a particular need. Providing such service for students with disabilities may require the media specialist to learn about, acquire, or develop new materials, techniques, and abilities, but in essence it is the same service they provide to all students. In fact, library media specialists are probably better prepared than many other teachers to do this, since they are charged with providing all types of media and technology to the school community. Technology, in fact, is one area which brings all three roles together. The library media specialist should provide information about available technologies which can help students with disabilities, teach the use of such technology, and, as instructional consultant, recommend appropriate technology to teachers and students. Furthermore, many people with disabilities use technology extensively and are very knowledgeable about it. Such people would make good staff members and student assistants in the library media center.

The last area I would like to mention in regard to the opportunities and possibilities presented by the ADA is forming partnerships. *Information Power* strongly emphasizes the need to build partnerships with others. Partnerships are mutual relationships; each partner should provide something to the other. The increased emphasis on people with disabilities which the ADA will engender will present many opportunities and possibilities for partnerships to the alert library media specialist. Although the term was not explicitly used, several types of partnerships with educators, students, and parents have already been described. Several other groups are productive partners. Library media specialists should form partnerships with organizations for people with disabilities, their parents, and their advocates. Such groups can supply information to media specialists about disabling conditions and appropriate ways to interact with people who are disabled. Each partner will be able to provide information about useful resources of which the other is not aware. Library media specialists can refer children with disabilities to appropriate organizations. Library media specialists and representatives of the organizations can present joint programs to parents and educators. Governmental agencies that serve people with disabilities also make good partners, and the activities already mentioned can also be done with them. Vocational rehabilitation agencies are especially useful partners for library media centers. Local businesses and public accommodations offer other possibilities for partnerships. Many of them will for the first time be required to open their facilities and activities to people with disabilities. They will need information on the ADA, what to do, and how to do it. Libraries will have this information available. Although public libraries, rather than school library media centers, may seem the most likely agency to provide this information, there is no reason why the latter cannot do so. Especially in small communities where the public library may not be well-equipped or staffed, educators may have more experience dealing with the situation. Offering to help local establishments striving to comply with the ADA could lead to interesting and potentially valuable partnerships.

## SUMMARY

Over the last quarter-century, a number of federal laws have mandated equal employment opportunities and accessible facilities and programs for people with disabilities in most schools in the United States. Because of these laws, almost all of the stipulations of the Americans with Disabilities Act of 1990 (ADA) are already in effect in most schools. Therefore, the ADA will have little direct impact upon school library media centers. However, as the law again brings the issue of disability rights to public consciousness, there will be indirect effects. This public awareness will also present many opportunities for school library media specialists to serve in informational and educational capacities with a variety of people and organizations.

## REFERENCES

1. National Council on Disability, *The Education of Students with Disabilities* (Washington, DC: GPO,1989).

2. National Information Center for Children and Youth with Disabilities, *The Education of Children and Youth with Special Needs: What Do the Laws Say? News Digest 1* (1991):1.

3. Ibid: 1-2.

4. Frederick J. Weintraub and Bruce A. Ramirez, *Progress in the Education of the Handicapped and Analysis of PL 98-199: The Education of the Handicapped Act Amendments of 1983* (Reston,VA:Council for Exceptional Children, 1985): 3.

5. National Advisory Committee on the Handicapped, *The Unfinished Revolution: Education for the Handicapped* (Washington, DC: GPO, 1976):3.

6. Ruth A. Velleman, *Meeting the Needs of People with Disabilities: A Guide for Librarians, Educators and Other Service Professionals* (Phoenix, AZ: Oryx, 1990):128.

7. National Advisory Committee on the Handicapped, 1976: 3.

8. 347 U.S. 483 (1954).

9. U.S. Constitution, Amendment XIV.

10. Laura F. Rothstein, *Special Education Law* (New York: Longman, 1990): 2.

11. Mary Helen Mahar, "Office of Education Support of School Media Programs," *Journal of Research and Development in Education* (1982)16:19-25.

12. Ibid.

13. Ibid.

14. National Information Center for Children and Youth with Disabilities, 1991: 2.

15. National Council on Disability, 1989: v.

16. Elementary and Secondary Education Act Amendments of 1968.

17. National Information Center for Children and Youth with Disabilities, 1991: 3.

18. Quoted by National Advisory Committee on the Handicapped, 1976: 4.

19. Ibid., 4.

20. Rehabilitation Act of 1973, Public Law 93-112.

21. Ibid.

22. Ibid.

23. William L. Needham and Gerald Jahoda, *Improving Library Service to Physically Disabled Persons: A Self-evaluation Checklist* (Littleton, CO: Libraries Unlimited, 1983): 105.

24. Education for All Handicapped Children Act of 1975, Public Law 94-142.

25. Ibid.

26. Rothstein, 1990: 295.

27. Velleman, 1990: 131.

28. Rothstein, 1990: 70.

29. National Information Center for Children and Youth with Disabilities, 1991: 6.

30. Ibid.

31. Americans with Disabilities Act of 1990 (ADA), (42 *USC* 12132).

32. ADA Regulations (28 *CFR* Part 35).

33. Ibid.

34. ADA Regulations (28 *CFR* Part 36).

35. Ibid.

36. Ibid.

37. Ibid.

38. Jane Jarrow, "Issues on Campus and the Road to ADA," *Educational Record* (1991) 72: 26-31.

39. Michael Peterson, "Models of Vocational Assessment of Handicapped Students," *American Annals of the Deaf* (1989) 134: 273-76.

40. ADA Regulations (28 *CFR* Part 35).

41. Jarrow, 1991: 28.

# CHAPTER 4
# The Americans with Disabilities Act: The Legal Implications

## PETER MANHEIMER

How much will I have to spend to make our library physically accessible?

Will we have to order books in Braille, large print, and audiotape?

Will we have to obtain videotapes and films in closed captioned versions?

Will we have to reduce the height of the bookshelves?

Will we have to hire persons with disabilities?

*Answers:* It depends. Perhaps. Possibly. No. Maybe.

You are now saying that these answers provide no answer at all and why should you read any further if this is the type of information you will receive. The reason that the answers are vague is because the Americans with Disabilities Act of 1990 (ADA) does not provide a one-size-fits-all solution to the complex issue of civil rights for persons with disabilities. There is a built-in flexibility to allow individual rights to be balanced against the needs and resources of the public or private sector service provider or employer. The purpose of this chapter is to provide the reader with guidelines to help understand the complexities of the ADA.

Although this chapter contains a discussion of the legal aspects of this legislation, you are urged to consult with counsel if you are in doubt as to whether you are in compliance with the law. As will be noted, state and local laws may alter your liabilities under the ADA.

As it is not possible to detail those laws in this chapter, you must seek competent advice on the implications of the law.

The Americans with Disabilities Act of 1990 became law on July 26, 1990. Various federal agencies and boards have been charged with drafting regulations interpreting the Act. The ADA consists of five parts or titles. Title I covers Employment; Title II, Public Services; Title III, Public Accommodations; Title IV, Telecommunications; and Title V contains miscellaneous provisions relating to certain exemptions, regulations, and enforcement. The Act, regulations, and judicial and administrative rulings will define how the ADA is to be applied.

In order to deal effectively with the Americans with Disabilities Act, it is helpful to consider the objective of the law; " . . . the elimination [of] discrimination against persons with disabilities."[1] The ADA is not intended to provide special privileges nor is it an affirmative action statute. It is expected that the ADA will be used to eliminate long-standing practices of discrimination.

Discrimination against persons with disabilities comes in many forms. There are of course blatant examples of prejudice ("We don't want those people here"). Discrimination can also take the form of paternalistic attitudes in which others decide that certain activities are beyond the abilities of or too strenuous or dangerous for a person with a disability. The most common form of discrimination is the type which occurs because society is not designed to accommodate people who are unable or find it difficult to walk, see, or hear. A building may be inaccessible because one must climb a flight of steps to reach the front door. Printed material can't be understood because it is not available in a format which can be read by a blind person and audio information is not generally provided to a deaf person in a manner which can be understood. While the last examples result from oversight and an historic lack of consideration for the needs of persons who are disabled, they bar individuals from the benefits of society just as surely as if one were to say "we don't want those people here."

Who is a person with a disability? The ADA definition has three parts. A disability is "a physical or mental impairment that substantially limits one or more major life activities . . . a record of such impairment; or being regarded as having such an impairment."[2] The first part of this definition defines disability on the basis of its effect on an individual rather than the physical manifestations of the condition which results in the disability. A limitation on one's ability to walk, see, hear, work, and/or attend school would be the type of limitation envisioned in the definition. The issue of how severe the limitation must be before it is considered a disability is subject to the existing circumstances. Although a broken toe would limit one's ability to walk, the relatively minor and temporary nature of such a limitation would not qualify one as being disabled under the ADA. This is not to say that permanence of a condition is a prerequisite to being considered disabled, but it would be one of the factors used to determine if there is a substantial limitation on life activities.

Disabling conditions are not limited to those which require use of wheelchairs or affect sight or hearing. Conditions which would generally be considered to cause a substantial limitation on major life activities include learning disabilities; psychological conditions; chronic illnesses such as cancer, heart or lung diseases, or AIDS; or alcoholism and drug abuse.

In keeping with prevailing attitudes on substance abuse, the ADA, while recognizing addictions as being a disabling condition, establish specific exemptions relating to drug use. Active drug use may be a basis to deny employment. One may also deny an active alcohol or drug user employment or services if the condition is such that it interferes with one's ability to perform the essential functions of the job or if such behavior would interrupt the function of a business. If an employee comes to work in a state of intoxication, the employer has the right to discipline or discharge the employee. If an alcoholic entered a library in an inebriated condition and proceeded to cause a disturbance (mere inebriation itself would not be a disturbance, but the person would have to be interfering with others' use of the facility), that person could be removed without violating his or her rights under the ADA. Removal would have to be based on the patron's inebriation and interference with other persons, not on the patron's alcoholism.

The second part of the definition of disability (a record of such impairment) covers situations in which a person experiences discrimination as a result of having been disabled (having a physical or mental impairment which substantially limits one or more major life activities) but is no longer affected by the disabling condition. A person whose cancer is in remission will often be denied employment because the prospective employer fears that the prior condition will have an adverse effect on insurance rates or the applicant's job performance. Similarly, many persons who have experienced psychological episodes, but have been treated and are no longer affected by such problems, suffer continued discrimination. In the above example of the alcoholic removed from the library because of his or her state of inebriation and the disturbance it caused, to deny that person, when sober, admission to the library in the future because of his or her history of alcohol abuse would be a violation of the ADA. The ADA protects this class of people from continued discrimination.

The last category involves persons who are regarded as having such an impairment. This section of the definition covers persons who do not have and have never had a physical or mental impairment that substantially limits one or more major life activities, but are perceived by others as having a disability. One of the more common examples of this part of the definition would be a person who has been burned on a visible portion of his or her body and is severely scarred as a result. Although the scarring would not necessarily interfere with the person's ability to walk, see, hear, or perform job or educational functions, society may view that person as being disabled and may discriminate against him or her as a result. This portion of the definition also protects persons who experience discrimination as a result of their relationship or association with persons who have a disability. One cannot bar a nurse who works in a hospice serving AIDS patients from using public services or accommodations because others fear he or she may be HIV positive. A person who has a child with Down's syndrome can't be denied employment because the potential employer believes that the child's needs will interfere with the applicant's ability to do the job.

The ADA definition of disability covers a multitude of circumstances in which discrimination against persons with disabilities occurs. This legislation seeks to protect all classes of persons from overt and subtle forms of bias.

## EMPLOYMENT

For libraries, the primary area of concern is how the ADA will affect a library's obligations to its patrons, but it is also important to examine a library's obligations as an employer, which are covered by Title I of the ADA.[3]

### Unemployment Rate

Persons with disabilities experience an unemployment rate which is significantly higher than the general population of the United States. While a national unemployment rate in excess of 7% is considered one indication of economic distress, the unemployment rate among working age persons with disabilities is approximately 60%. Subgroups, such as African-American women with disabilities, experience even higher rates of unemployment. Surveys also show that among unemployed persons with disabilities, two-thirds express a desire to work. While there are many reasons, other than bias, as to why the unemployment rates are distressingly high, the ADA is intended to provide a legal guideline to eliminate discrimination which contributes to this national problem. The ADA addresses overt discrimination ("we don't want them here"), paternalistic discrimination ("we are afraid they can't do the job even though they seem willing to try"), and discrimination caused by circumstances ("we just aren't equipped to meet their needs").

Those of you who work in the public sector are not (or should not be) unfamiliar with antidiscrimination laws which protect the employment rights of people with disabilities. Libraries which, directly or indirectly, are the recipients of federal funding have been covered by the mandates of the Rehabilitation Act of 1973. Additionally, over the years you may have been subject to various state or local laws which are intended to protect the civil rights of persons with disabilities. While we would like to say that this earlier legislation has addressed the employment issue to such an extent that the impact of the ADA is minimal, this is not the case. The antidiscrimination provisions of the Rehabilitation Act of 1973 were not as clearly defined as those found in the ADA. Unless a library was an instrumentality of the federal government, one had to trace federal funding to determine if Section 504 of the Rehabilitation Act of 1973 covered that entity. Originally, all agencies of a state or local government which received U.S. funds came under the requirements of Section 504 of the Rehabilitation Act of 1973 in their entirety. This changed with the U.S. Supreme Court decision of *Grove City College v. Bell*,[4] which only held those specific programs of a state or local government which received funding to be liable under Section 504 of the Rehabilitation Act of 1973. In 1988, Congress extended coverage back to its original status with the passage of the Civil Rights Restoration Act.

The ADA will eliminate the need to trace funds to the federal government in order to determine coverage. It refines the definitions of who is covered, both as employers and employees; what considerations must be made in hiring a person with a disability; and what type of job accommodations may be required. The ADA is also more specific in its enforcement provisions and gives an aggrieved person the right to pursue his or her claim through arbitration, administrative action, or private lawsuit. One does not have to exhaust his or her administrative remedies before filing an individual lawsuit.

Bear in mind that the ADA is intended to eliminate discrimination which has existed over the years. It is not an affirmative action program. One does not have to hire an unqualified person merely because he or she has a disability in order to fill a predetermined number of employees from that class. It is the objective of the ADA to eliminate employment barriers which have kept large numbers of disabled persons out of the workplace.

Which employers are covered? All private employers who employ more than 25 employees are covered by the ADA as of July 26, 1992. On July 26, 1994, coverage will extend to employers who employ 15 or more employees, the same number set forth in the Civil Rights Act of 1964. A word of caution—state or local laws relating to discrimination in employment may extend protection to businesses employing a smaller number of employees. While state or local laws cannot reduce the coverage set forth in the ADA, state or local laws will govern if their provisions are more stringent than ADA requirements. Regulations interpreting the ADA have concluded that public employers are covered by Title I, regardless of the number of persons employed as of January 26, 1992. Specifically exempted from the requirements of Title I of the ADA are the United States, a wholly owned corporation of the U.S. (the federal government as an employer, is covered by the provisions of the Rehabilitation Act of 1973), Indian tribes, and tax exempt private membership clubs (other than labor organizations).[5] Religious organizations may also give preference in hiring to members of their own religion, even if a job applicant with a disability may be more qualified than a job applicant who is a member of that religious group.[6] If you are in doubt whether you are covered, consult competent counsel.

Who is protected under the ADA? The ADA is intended to provide protection against employment discrimination to qualified individuals with a disability. In order to meet the ADA requirements, an employer must determine if the job applicant is qualified and whether he or she can perform the essential functions of the job with or without reasonable accommodations.

Is the applicant qualified? The first thing that an employer should do to answer this question is to examine job descriptions and requirements. While the ADA does not generally require an employee to have a written job description (check to see if state and local laws have such requirements), it is a good practice to have them. Make sure your stated requirements actually relate to what an employee will need to do on the job and do not unduly discriminate against persons with disabilities. Many places of employment require all employees to possess a valid driver's license. Unless driving a motor vehicle is an essential function of the job, such a requirement would operate to discriminate against persons whose disability prevents them from driving. These driver's license requirements are usually used (in nondriving employment situations) as a means of identification and that need can be satisfied by requiring proof of identification in forms other than a driver's license.

## Job Requirements

Job requirements must relate to the work expected and cannot be arbitrary. Several years ago, many places of business had height and weight restrictions for their employees. Police and fire departments imposed such restrictions on the theory that they had a direct correlation to the physical strength needed to carry out the job. Those restrictions operated to discriminate against women who could not meet the qualifications and they were challenged under a series of gender discrimination cases. Evidence showed that height and weight standards did not correlate to any necessary job function and they were consequently eliminated. Review your job descriptions to eliminate requirements which tend to discriminate against persons with disabilities unless you can show that the restriction is essential to job performance.

Restrictive job requirements will continue to be permitted under the ADA if they relate to job necessities. You will be free to require that job applicants for a librarian position have a master's degree from an American Library Association accredited program if that is considered to be necessary in your particular system. If an applicant for such a position has a disability but does not hold those qualifications, you will be free to deny him or her that position. This is true even if the applicant would contend that he or she could not meet those requirements because of a disability. That applicant would not be considered qualified for the job.

What happens if an applicant with a disability meets the minimum job qualifications, but another applicant who is not disabled has better qualifications? Must we hire the person who is disabled? Remember the ADA is not an affirmative action law. An employer is entitled to select the best qualified applicant. However, the superior qualifications of one applicant as opposed to another must relate to the job. The superior candidate for the job of research librarian must be considered superior because of greater experience or scholarship not because he or she is a championship tennis player.

What will happen if two applicants have equal qualifications? Can we hire the one who is not disabled? Again the answer is yes. However, this presents a more difficult situation, particularly if you are called upon to justify your decision. Ask yourself: Why have I selected the candidate without the disability? Unless you can convince yourself that there is a valid and legally justifiable reason you may have difficulty convincing others that you were not motivated by bias. This is difficult because there are certain intangibles in the hiring process; sometimes you just have a gut feeling that one applicant will work out better than another. Of course if you have a good record of hiring persons with disabilities at all job levels in your facility (not just as custodians), you will have greater latitude in making choices among equally qualified candidates.

### Essential Functions

What is meant by being able to perform the essential functions of the job? This goes back to your review of your job description and requirements. Are there job duties that have been done in the past which are incidental to the job but could serve to render an applicant with a disability as unqualified? If so, those duties may have to be modified or reassigned. If a job applicant who uses a wheelchair is seeking a position as a secretary and if the current secretary occasionally covers for the file clerk, a duty which the applicant would not be able to perform, you must ask if the file clerk coverage aspects are essential and if they can be eliminated or transferred from the secretarial duties without creating an "undue hardship" ("significant difficulty or expense").[7]

The amount of time spent on this duty is but one factor to consider. The occasional nature of the duty may indicate that it is not essential. Other factors which should be considered are whether there are others who can preform this duty in the file clerk's absence without substantially interfering with their other duties or if the work can be left until the file clerk returns. Obviously, a larger facility would have greater flexibility in reassigning incidental duties, and if this is the case, this type of duty would not be considered essential and must not serve as a bar to employment.

By way of example, we can look to a case decided under the Rehabilitation Act of 1973. An applicant for a position as a registered nurse in a Veterans Administration (VA) hospital was a recovered drug user (active drug use is not a covered disability in an employment situation either under the Rehabilitation Act of 1973 or the ADA) and she met all job qualifications. However, her physician advised her not to handle or administer narcotic drugs. The VA hospital determined that one of the job requirements was to administer narcotic drugs to patients and, as the applicant was unable to do so, she was denied the position. In subsequent proceedings, it was found that the administration of narcotic drugs was a relatively small portion of the duties of a registered nurse at that hospital (about 2% of the total job time) and that it was common practice for nurses to trade duties for a variety of reasons. It was determined that the administration of narcotic drugs was an incidental function of the job and that the duty could be assumed by others without substantial interference with the overall operation of the hospital and was a reasonable accommodation. Therefore the denial of the position was an act of discrimination.[8]

Of course there are certain job requirements which would be deemed essential and if one's disability prevented him or her from executing those duties, he or she would not be considered qualified. Going back to the applicant for the secretarial position, if he or she were instead to apply for the position of file clerk, the act of filing would be essential, and if the applicant's disability prevented him or her from doing the work, a job offer need not be made. Although the library can't require all job applicants to possess a driver's license, it is appropriate to require an applicant for a position as driver of a bookmobile to meet such a requirement because driving is an essential function of the job. Clearly, a blind applicant cannot perform the essential functions required of a driver of a bookmobile.

The key to meeting the essential-function-of-the-job test is to be flexible. Even if an incidental duty has been customarily done by an employee in one position, if it serves to render an applicant who can't do that duty unqualified, you must consider eliminating that task or transferring it to another if this can be done without creating an undue hardship.

## Reasonable Accommodations

What is meant by performing the essential function of the job with or without reasonable accommodations? Many persons with disabilities can perform in the job place, but require certain modifications to the workplace or schedule, assistance or specialized equipment in order to do so. If a job is beyond the ability of an applicant, the applicant may not be denied employment if the job can be done with the assistance of a reasonable accommodation.

Reasonable accommodations come in many forms. The reassignment of nonessential job functions is one such accommodation. Modification of the job place (e.g., placing a desk on blocks so that a person in a wheelchair can get the chair under it or placing files used by that person in a lower file cabinet drawer) is another. Personal assistance (e.g., having another employee answer the telephone for a deaf employee) would qualify as an accommodation. New technologies (telephone amplifiers, enlarged displays or voice synthesizers on computers, text enlarging or reading equipment, Telecommunication Devices for the Deaf or TDDs) have greatly expanded the job capabilities of persons with disabilities and are one type of reasonable accommodation.

If an otherwise qualified job applicant with a disability cannot perform the essential functions of a job as structured, but can perform the job with the addition of a reasonable accommodation, and if the provision of the reasonable accommodation will not be an undue hardship for the employer, the denial of the job would be deemed discriminatory unless there is a more qualified applicant. Although an employer can deny the accommodation if it would create an undue hardship and therefore deny employment if the applicant cannot otherwise perform the essential functions of the job, the employer cannot consider the cost of the accommodation as a basis for hiring if the provision of the accommodation does not cause an undue hardship. If a job applicant with a disability needs an accommodation which requires a onetime expenditure of $1,000, which would not be an undue hardship on the employer, and if the employer elected to hire an equally qualified applicant who is not disabled because it would not have to spend the extra money for the nondisabled applicant, the employer has discriminated under the ADA. The cost of a reasonable accommodation which does not create an undue hardship cannot be a factor in the hiring process.

Now that you are thoroughly frightened it is comforting to know that estimates on the cost of reasonable accommodations bring them well within the capabilities of most employers. The cost of placing the desk on blocks to accommodate the employee who uses a wheelchair is negligible; it costs nothing to move files to a lower file cabinet drawer or reassign some job tasks. An amplified receiver on a telephone is less than $100 and TDDs can be purchased for under $300. Of course there are more costly accommodations. Structural changes to the physical plant (installation of elevators, making doors wider for restroom accessibility, and installation of ramps) can be expensive. However, many of these modifications, which may be required for employees under Title I, are also going to apply to obligations to the patrons under Titles II and III, but more on that later. Remember, if a structural modification would create an undue hardship, the employer can relocate the work site as an accommodation. If an employee who supervises the ordering of periodicals has been occupying an inaccessible second floor office, and if an applicant for the job would not be able to get to the office, there are options. The existing office can be made accessible, if that does not result in an undue hardship or the office can be relocated to an accessible location.

### Accommodations and Undue Hardships

How do I know what kind of accommodation is needed? The best source of information is usually the person who needs the accommodation. You must be careful in pre-job offer interviews not to inquire about a person's disability but you can inquire how the applicant will accomplish the essential duties of the job. There will be more on this later. If he or she is unsure of what is needed, technical assistance can be provided by public and private agencies. The potential employee's request does not require the employer to provide the requested accommodation. A deaf employee may prefer to use a $1,500 TDD but if a $250 TDD will allow the applicant to perform the duties of the job, the employer is free to acquire the less expensive equipment. An accommodation must also be reasonable. While it would be reasonable to move files to a lower file cabinet drawer to accommodate the secretary who uses a wheelchair, it is not reasonable for the blind applicant for the position of bookmobile driver to demand that another employee assume all the driving tasks of the job.

The term undue hardship, meaning an action requiring significant difficulty or expense, has been mentioned a number of times. What exactly does this mean? The ADA does not specifically define undue hardship other than referring to significant difficulty or expense. This is because what is a hardship for a small municipal library may not be a hardship for an academic library at a major public or private university. However, there are some guidelines to be considered. The nature and cost of the accommodation, overall financial resources, number of employees, overall impact on operations, nature of business, structure and function of the workforce, etc. are all factors considered in determining whether a hardship exists.[9] Use common sense in determining if the accommodation creates an undue hardship. A facility which is faced with either providing an accommodation or laying off an essential part-time employee is in a good position to claim undue hardship. However, if your library is purchasing $25,000 in new computer equipment but claims it can't afford a $350 computer program to enlarge the video display for an employee with limited vision, it is going to have a tough time claiming undue hardship. A large library with many employees is likely to be in a position to transfer certain duties which cannot be accomplished by an employee with a disability; a small library may not have that flexibility.

The determination of what is or is not an undue hardship is a question of fact that will be decided on a case-to-case basis. Administrative and judicial decisions evaluating claims of undue hardship will provide additional guidance as to what this term means. Although it may be too early to tell, given the intent of the ADA, benefits of the doubt will likely be decided in favor of the job seeker and not the employer. The keyword in the definition is "substantial." If the provision of an accommodation causes mere inconvenience, it is unlikely to be considered a significant difficulty. One should not anticipate using the undue hardship exemption as a means of avoiding the provision of reasonable accommodations or hiring an applicant with a disability unless the hardship truly exists.

### Disability Inquiry

If a job applicant has a disability, may he or she be asked about a disability on the employment application or in a job interview? The ADA does not permit inquiry into a person's disability at either the application or interview stage. In addition, pre-offer medical inquiries or examinations are prohibited under the law.[10] An employer may inquire into the ability of an employee to perform job-related functions, but not the disability itself.[11] It would be illegal for an employer to ask the prospective employee how he or she became disabled and how that affects his or her outlook on life. It is acceptable to ask a blind applicant how they will access a computer if doing so is an essential job function.

After a job offer is made, the employer may make medical inquiry or require a medical examination and may condition the offer of employment on the results of such inquiry or examination. However, this may be done only if all entering employees are subject to a post-offer medical inquiry and if the results are kept confidential and disclosed only on a need-to-know basis.[12] A job offer may be withdrawn on the basis of the results of the medical inquiry only if the reason for withdrawing the offer is job-related and consistent with business necessity.[13] If a post-offer eye examination of an applicant offered a job as a bookmobile driver reveals that his or her corrected vision is less acute than what is allowable by the state motor vehicle department as a condition for holding a driver's license, the job offer can be withdrawn. However, if the results show that the applicant had a history of cancer, the job offer may not be withdrawn merely because the employer is concerned that the employee may experience a high rate of absenteeism or because it is feared that the group medical insurance rates may increase as a result of covering that employee.

Who is not covered under the ADA? It has already been mentioned that religious organizations may give preference in hiring to members of their own religion. A person with a disability would not be covered if the reason he or she was not hired was due to religious preference rather than disability. Also mentioned is the specific exemption for active use of illegal drugs. Although drug dependency is considered a disability in other sections of the ADA, active drug use or on-the-job alcohol intoxication can be a basis for denial of or termination of employment. Testing for illegal drug use is exempted from the medical examination restrictions of Title I of the ADA. Further specifics relating to drug use are set forth in Title V, which also states that the definition of disability shall not include homosexuality, bisexuality, transvestism, transsexualism, pedophilia, exhibitionism, voyeurism, gender identity disorders, sexual behavior disorders, compulsive gambling, kleptomania, or pyromania.[14] If a person has one or more of these conditions and is otherwise disabled, he or she is still entitled to the protection of the ADA based upon the existence of the disability as opposed to the exempt condition.

### Employment Protection Other Than in the Hiring Process

Does the ADA affect areas other than the initial employment process and the provision of accommodations to a newly hired employee? The ADA covers all employees, including employees who have a disability but were hired before the effective date of the ADA and those employees who have become disabled after they were hired. The ADA also covers all aspects of the job. If an employee becomes disabled after the time he or she was hired, the employer would be required to provide him or her with reasonable accommodations to allow the employee to remain on the job. If the extent of the disabling condition would cause an existing employee to be unable to perform the essential functions of the job with or without reasonable accommodations, the employee may be considered unqualified for the job and may be discharged.

In addition to protection against discrimination in the hiring process, a person with a disability is covered under Title I in connection with ". . . advancement, discharge . . ., employee compensation, job training, and other terms, conditions and privileges of employment."[15] This means that an employer can not treat an employee with a disability differently from other employees. Not only must the work station be accessible, but the employee lounge and cafeteria must also be available to the employee who has a disability.

### Position Benefits

One of the more difficult issues under the ADA is the provision of benefits, specifically insurance for the employee with a disability. While the employer can not discriminate against an employee, Title V permits insurers and similar organizations and entities to set insurance rates and coverage in a manner which is acceptable under various state insurance laws and regulations. This means that insurers will be allowed to rate persons with disabilities at a higher premium scale, exclude certain coverage, or deny coverage altogether if such practice is permitted by a state's insurance regulations. Title V states that this allowance for insurance cannot be used to avoid obligations under Titles I and III.[16]

Because of the insurance provisions, it is difficult to predict how unequal treatment of a person with a disability will be addressed regarding insurance as a job benefit. It appears that an employer can't deny a person with a disability employment merely because the insurance rates will increase, unless it can be shown that the increase will result in an undue hardship to the employer. What is not so apparent is what will happen in cases where the employee with a disability is required to pay more for insurance than other employees. It is also not clear what will happen if exemptions to a policy render the value of the policy to be less than what is given to other employees or if coverage is totally denied. Will the employer be expected to pick up the extra expense assessed against the employee with a disability? Will the employer be required to provide the employee with additional compensation or alternative benefits to make up for unavailable or lesser insurance coverage? Will the employer be required to place its insurance with a company which does not treat employees with a disability differently from other employees? The answers to these questions, if they currently exist, lie with the state insurance regulators and we can expect to see some administrative and judicial decisions in the future clarifying the respective rights and liabilities of employers and employees in connection with insurance coverage.

Library directors may not have considered this aspect of the ADA, but it is an extremely important part of the law. Because of the financial impact of employment on both the employer and employee, the requirements of Title I may have greater impact on the operation of libraries than issues concerning service to library patrons.

## PUBLIC SERVICES

Title II of the Americans with Disabilities Act of 1990 covers Public Services. Title II will govern many libraries' duties to their patrons. A public entity is "any State or local government" and "any department, agency, special purpose district, or other instrumentality of a State or States or local government . . . ."[17] Once again, departments, agencies, or instrumentalities of the United States government are excluded from coverage by the ADA, although they continue to be covered by the provisions of the Rehabilitation Act of 1973. In other words, all public libraries, public school libraries, public college and university academic libraries, and special libraries which are part of a public entity (a court's law library or a health department's medical library) are subject to the requirements of Title II of the ADA.

Title II is divided into two subtitles. Subtitle A is very short and says ". . . no qualified individual with a disability shall, by reason of such disability, be excluded from participation in or be denied the benefits of the services, programs, or activities of a public entity, or be subjected to discrimination by any such entity."[18] A public entity's responsibility under this Subtitle is essentially governed by the provisions of Section 504 of the Rehabilitation Act of 1973 and the regulations promulgated under that law. Although the provisions of the Rehabilitation Act of 1973 are not as detailed as those of the ADA, we must look to the regulations issued under that law as well as those issued under the ADA to determine the extent of the law. Subtitle A has an effective date of January 26, 1992. Subtitle B, which comprises the bulk of Title II, relates to Public Transportation. While there are some circumstances in which a library may be affected by the Public Transportation provisions, it is not anticipated that this will be a major concern to most libraries and we will therefore concentrate on Subtitle A. Transportation considerations will be discussed, in brief, later in this chapter.

## Access

Once again we should look to the overall intent of the legislation in order to give perspective to the requirements. It is intended that persons with disabilities have full and complete access to public facilities and programs. This means that libraries, as structures, should be made accessible and that a library's collection and library-sponsored programs should also be made accessible. This presents serious concerns for libraries because the costs of access can be high. Since most libraries covered under Title II of the ADA have been covered by Section 504 of the Rehabilitation Act of 1973, many access issues should have been addressed before now. Nevertheless, the reality is that many facilities and the services provided within them are less than accessible.

The problem of physical access is more likely to affect older facilities. Newer buildings, as a general rule, would have been constructed in accordance with more modern state and local building codes which contain access provisions. Part of the reason older buildings have not reached the desired state of access is due to allowances in Section 504 of the Rehabilitation Act of 1973 for the provision of alternative services in lieu of direct access. Many libraries opted to deliver services at alternative, accessible locations or by mail or bookmobile, rather than renovate older inaccessible facilities. This practice was probably overused as a method of complying with Section 504 of the Rehabilitation Act of 1973 because the section's intent was to allow that exemption for small providers and it was not intended as an across-the-board substitute for general access. The regulations promulgated under Section 504 of the Rehabilitation Act of 1973 and overall enforcement were not as strong as we might expect to see under the ADA. If we consider the overall intent of the ADA as bringing persons with disabilities into the mainstream of society, we can anticipate that attempts to use alternative means of service delivery, in lieu of full access, will be restricted to circumstances in which the provision of full access is either extremely difficult or expensive.

One of the ways libraries have addressed the issues of physical access and access to their collections has been the establishment of centralized services and locations to serve the needs of persons with disabilities. In larger systems, the main library may have been made physically accessible and the system's collection of Braille and audiotaped materials may have been housed in that location. However, branch libraries might have remained physically inaccessible and a patron who needed material in alternative media could only use the branch library to order material from the main library. While this may have been acceptable under Section 504 of the Rehabilitation Act of 1973, it is likely that the ADA will require greater access in the branch facilities. When one considers the equities of the situations, the general library patron is given the option of using any branch or the main facility, as he or she desires. The philosophy of the ADA would require that patrons with disabilities be afforded the same choice whenever possible.

## Undue Financial Burden

What happens if the budget does not allow full physical access to all facilities? Where Title I allows exemptions based upon undue hardship, Title II refers to undue financial burden. The differences between these two terms is that the former also allows for exemption if there is an administrative burden while the latter does not. Obviously the financial burden exemption may be used when budget constraints do not allow full access. In those cases, alternative program access must be provided by having an alternative accessible facility, Books-by-Mail, or other reasonable alternatives to the lack of physical access. One must also keep in mind that budgets (and budget constraints) are ongoing factors in any operation. One cannot rely on such an exemption indefinitely when access can be provided in stages. Let us assume that the cost of renovating a facility to provide access is $100,000. If the annual budget will only allow for a $10,000 expenditure, one should begin applying that money to remove physical barriers in stages rather than ignoring the problem because it can't be completely corrected within one fiscal year. Barrier removal which is to be done in stages should begin from the outside and work in. Start with parking and entrance accessibility. Move on to make the most frequently used areas accessible and leave the less used areas for last. Along the way, remember that facilities such as restrooms, drinking fountains, circulation desks, and public telephones also must be accessible.

While renovations to existing facilities can be costly, there is no excuse for inaccessible new facilities. Although current building codes require access, don't assume that the plans as presented will provide the needed access. Too often architects view projects in the light of aesthetic appeal and don't adequately consider the needs of the users. The building may meet minimum code standards for access and still be difficult to use. Review plans through the eyes of a person with a disability. Does one have to negotiate a series of corridors and doorways to get to the elevator? Does the decorative fountain or landscaping unduly increase the distance one has to travel from the parking lot to the front door? While aesthetics are important, be sure your facilities are user friendly.

We have limited space. Do we have to place all of our books and materials within arms reach of all patrons? The answer is no. It is recognized that reduction of shelf height would require unreasonable increases in required floor space or reductions of collections. However, there should be adequate space between stacks (36 inches minimum, 42 inches preferred) to allow a person who uses a wheelchair to move down an aisle and staff must be available to assist patrons who can't get to materials which are out of arm's reach. Obviously, collections which are intended primarily for the use of persons with disabilities should be accessible without the need for assistance. It is also suggested that frequently used materials (such as magazine displays and card catalogs) be placed so that they are accessible. When considering access to materials, also consider the placement of equipment. Online catalogs can resolve many problems persons with disabilities have in accessing the old card catalogs; however, if the computer terminal is placed at counter-top height, the advantage of this system is lost. Similarly, photocopiers and microfilm and fiche machines should be readily accessible.

## Alternative Formats and Assistive Devices

Do we have to purchase Braille, large print, and audiotape versions of every item acquired? Once again the answer is no. Alternative formats are available through the Library of Congress and other sources and every library should be prepared to assist clients requesting such materials. Although libraries will not be required to duplicate their print collections in alternative formats, such items should be acquired whenever possible. Once again, start such a collection with items which are most frequently used and items which are targeted for patrons who need alternatives to print. Technology will also assist libraries in extending their collections to persons who are unable to read standard printed material. Text enlarging equipment, text reading machines and computers with scanners, screen readers and voice synthesizers can provide access to collections for a relatively modest cost when compared with the expense of duplicating one's collection with alternative format material.

What do we need to do to serve deaf or hearing impaired patrons? Will we be required to have persons on staff who know sign language? The needs of persons who are deaf or hearing impaired are frequently overlooked. While it would be nice to have a staff member available who is familiar with sign language, the ADA will not require it in most instances for the day-to-day business of the library. However, all staff should be prepared to communicate with persons who are deaf or hearing impaired. Many persons with limited hearing can understand you if you speak clearly (don't shout) and look directly at them. Don't mumble or talk with your hand over your mouth. In other instances, pencil and paper or a convenient computer screen will be sufficient to allow you to communicate.

Title IV of the ADA will require telephone companies to establish a telephone relay system no later than July 1993 which will allow a person with hearing or speech limitations to communicate over the telephone by using the relay service as an intermediary. All libraries will need to purchase a Telecommunication Device for the Deaf (TDD, TTY, or text telephone) if not available by January 1992. These machines are relatively inexpensive and simple to operate. They will allow deaf patrons to call the library directly and obtain information just as any other patron may do. Merely having a TDD is useless if the TDD number is not published or if the staff does not know how to use it.

Deaf patrons will further be served if you purchase closed captioned video tapes whenever available rather than noncaptioned versions. Closed captioned decoders are also relatively inexpensive and easily within the budget of any library which offers video material. Don't forget that life safety items such as fire alarms should have visual as well as audible warnings.

## Alternative Service Delivery

In cases where full access is not possible because of financial burden, what guidelines must be followed in providing alternative program accessibility? There are no hard and fast rules to guide you in this area. The one thing which must be kept in mind is whether the alternative access is comparable. Comparable does not mean identical, but the further you get away from the level of service provided to the general population, the further you get from offering comparable service. One way of providing alternative service is to have material sent from an inaccessible facility to an accessible location. This would not be an acceptable method of alternate service delivery if it would take several weeks to get the material as opposed to having the material sent within a day or two. Making one library in a multifacility system accessible may be an acceptable alternative, if the patron would not have to travel an unreasonable distance and if the accessible facility was open during the same days and hours as other inaccessible libraries in the system. Books-by-Mail is another way to provide alternative service and, for some patrons, this may be the preferred method of receiving service. However, this should not be viewed as the exclusive method of alternative service delivery because it is not comparable to other library services.

Don't overlook access to library services and programs other than traditional book lending and research. If your library offers lectures and educational programs, they must be accessible to persons with disabilities. If these have been traditionally offered in a place with limited access, they should be moved to an accessible location. Unless it can be shown that such a move will cause an undue financial burden, alternative access (e.g., a videotape of the program) is not an acceptable substitute for physical access. Once again, physical access is not total access. While a library may not be required to have a sign language interpreter on staff to serve the regular library usage needs of deaf patrons, if a program (such as a lecture series) is offered, arrangements should be made for sign language interpretation on request, because pencil and paper notes will not take the place of hearing the entire presentation.

## Transportation

This is a good time to raise the issue of transportation access. As noted, the bulk of Title II relates to this very issue. Libraries are not in the business of transportation; however, if the public is offered transportation to a particular program or event, the transportation offered must be accessible to persons with disabilities, including persons who use wheelchairs. In the unlikely event a public library runs a fixed route system to transport people, meaning "a vehicle is operated along a prescribed route according to a fixed schedule,"[19] the library is required, as of August 26, 1990, to purchase or lease only accessible vehicles whenever a vehicle is purchased or leased. If such a route is operating with existing nonaccessible vehicles, both the ADA and Section 504 of the Rehabilitation Act of 1973 require that comparable transportation be offered to persons unable to access the traditional vehicles. Although there are exceptions to the transportation requirements other than the undue financial burden exception, because libraries are not likely to be public entities operating fixed route transportation systems, we will not discuss those circumstances.

If a library does occasionally offer transportation, it would more likely be considered a public entity operating a demand responsive system under Section 224 of the ADA. In that case, it must be shown that the " . . . system, when viewed in its entirety, provides a level of service to such individuals [persons with disabilities who can't access traditional transportation vehicles] equivalent to the level of service such system provides to individuals without disabilities."[20] In other words, one can purchase or lease nonaccessible vehicles if reasonable and comparable service is provided to persons who need alternative transportation.

Transportation, like other services which may not be considered the traditional business of a library, must take into consideration the needs of persons with disabilities in order to avoid a claim of discrimination under the ADA.

## PUBLIC ACCOMMODATIONS

While many public entities which are affected by Title II of the ADA should be somewhat familiar with antidiscrimination laws because of the effect of Section 504 of the Rehabilitation Act of 1973, private entities which are not the recipients of federal funding have generally not been faced with such requirements. Title III of the ADA addresses those entities. From the standpoint of libraries, Title III will affect private academic, institutional, and special libraries. Access to these facilities is mandated in the same way as public libraries are affected under Title II.

The primary difference between the Title II and Title III requirements is found in the exemption provisions. Access to facilities and programs must be provided under Title III if it is readily achievable. This is a lower standard than undue hardship under Title I or undue financial burden under Title II. "Readily achievable" is defined in

Section 301(9) as being " . . . easily accomplished and able to be carried out without much difficulty or expense."[21] This exemption gives private entities much greater latitude in deciding whether to make their facilities and programs accessible to everyone. Nevertheless, in determining whether an accommodation is "readily achievable" various factors will be considered such as the nature and cost of the action and the overall financial resources of the entity. Once again, larger and more financially secure entities will be required to expend greater efforts and resources than smaller enterprises. This is only equitable because the library in a major private university is in a better position to provide accommodations and access than a small rural public or school library even though those institutions come under the more stringent requirements of Title II.

In cases in which the private entity can demonstrate that provision of physical or program access is not readily achievable, alternative provision of services is required (delivery of materials by mail or to the curb). Once again, the expense commonly associated with renovation of existing facilities, which may give rise to a claim that such modification is not readily achievable, does not permit a private entity to construct a new facility which is inaccessible. Title III also specifies in Sections 302(1)(B) and (C) that services shall be provided in the most integrated setting possible and that persons with disabilities shall not be denied the right to participate in programs or services which are not separate or different from those offered to the general public.[22] We can see that even though exemptions are more easily obtained under Title III, the intent of the law is that persons with disabilities shall be able to enjoy the same rights as all other members of society. We can therefore expect that claims for exemptions under Title III will not be granted because of mere inconvenience or if modest expense is required.

The Americans with Disabilities Act of 1990 will have a significant impact on the lives of persons with disabilities. Society will have to make adjustments in order to effectuate the intent of this legislation. For those who have been in compliance with the requirements of Section 504 of the Rehabilitation Act of 1973, the changes will not be significant. Many have expressed fears as to the costs of complying. In all likelihood, most changes and accommodations will be small. There are adequate provisions for exceptions where the costs will create problems for providers. The fear of litigation will be minimized if those faced with compliance look on the ADA as being beneficial to society as a whole rather than looking for ways of avoiding the effect of the law. As noted, no legislation can magically change long-held beliefs and prejudices. Over a period of time the entrance of persons with disabilities into the mainstream of society will break down many of the attitudinal barriers which cause much of the apprehension which has been expressed over the ADA.

## REFERENCES

1. ADA, Section 2 (b)(1), 42 (*USC*)12101.

2. ADA, Section 3(2), 42 (*USC*)12102.

3. 104 *STAT.*330, Public Law 101-336.

4. 104 *S.Ct.* 121 (1984).

5. ADA, Section 101 (5) (B).

6. ADA, Section 103 (C).

7. ADA, Section 101 (10).

8. *Wallace v. Veterans Administration*, 683 *F.Supp.* 758 (*USDC Kan.* 1988).

9. ADA, Section 101 (10) (B).

10. ADA, Section 102(c)(2)(A).

11. ADA, Section 102(c)(2)(B).

12. ADA, Section 102(c)(3).

13. ADA, Section 102(c)(4)(A).

14. ADA, Section 511.

15. ADA, Section 102(a).

16. ADA, Section 501(c).

17. ADA, Section 201(1).

18. ADA, Section 202.

19. ADA, Section 221 (3).

20. ADA, Section 224.

21. ADA, Section 301(9).

22. ADA, Section 302(1) (B) and (C).

# CHAPTER 5
# ADA Case Studies and Exercises

## DONALD D. FOOS AND NANCY C. PACK

### INTRODUCTION

This series of purely hypothetical and theoretical (and possibly bizarre) case studies was developed to apply the ADA to situations that academic, public, school, and special libraries might face. A cast of typical characters was created for the case studies, and a number of question-and-answer exercises were devised to test the application of the ADA in these settings.

Since the ADA was enacted only recently (July 26, 1990), it has not been tested in the courts. This is especially important for the compliance requirements, which become effective on July 26, 1992, for employers with 25 or more employees, and on July 26, 1994, for employers with 15-24 employees (*see* Appendix B, "Americans with Disabilities Act Statutory Deadlines"). Under the statutory deadlines of the ADA, generally, lawsuits under Title III may not be filed until January 26, 1992. It may be assumed that other types of lawsuits and related activities would have to be filed after each respective compliance date of the ADA.

Readers will find these case studies useful as graphic illustrations of the ADA and its application. As vigilant consumer groups with disabilities become increasingly active, libraries, especially public libraries, will likely become priority targets for their activities.

### CASE 1: THE NEW DEPUTY DIRECTOR

After 15 years of advancing through various professional library positions in medium-sized public libraries, Donna Winmore (holder of an MLS) is the newly appointed deputy director of a large public library system. During the transition period between jobs, the Americans with Disabilities Act of 1990 was signed. Upon reporting to her new library, Ms. Winmore enters an orientation session with the library's director, Emma Hardnose. Ms. Hardnose has been in her position for 25 years, having received her BLS (the former American Library Association accredited library science degree awarded prior to 1956, as the fifth year degree) in 1955. She is planning to retire in three years.

Ms. Hardnose, a local hometown person, and a long-ago president of the state's library association, has gradually disassociated herself from professional involvements in any type of library or related association. Her professional reading is nil, and she now spends most of her time (at home) reading about her longtime hobby, advanced linen tatting.

During the late 1960s, the library received grant funds from Title II (Construction) of the Library Services and Construction Act to build branch libraries. As the library system's deputy director at that time, Ms. Hardnose was responsible for the internal management of federal funds for the library's system. She also oversaw the library's compliance under the Civil Rights Act of 1964.

As a strong advocate of library and information science current awareness, and an upwardly mobile person, Ms. Winmore is aware of all newly enacted federal legislation related to libraries. She knows the ADA and its regulations and guidelines, inside and out. Ten minutes into the orientation session with Ms. Hardnose, Ms. Winmore asks about the library system's plans to implement and comply with the ADA.

Ms. Hardnose asks, "What's ADA? The state library agency hasn't mentioned anything about it." (The state library agency has a slightly older contemporary of Ms. Hardnose as state librarian.)

Knowing that she's in an at-will library position, Ms. Winmore gently briefs Ms. Hardnose on the ADA and its regulations and guidelines especially as they relate to the library's particular situation. She tells her that the ADA's Title I requirements become effective on July 26, 1992 and Title II requirements on January 26, 1992. Ms. Hardnose remembered that the library's compliance under Section 504 of the Rehabilitation Act of 1973 was monitored by the state library agency (only state libraries were required to file compliances), and she didn't think that an ADA compliance would now be necessary or required.

Ms. Winmore is now in a self-imposed dilemma. She knows that the ADA will apply to the library and that the library will have to comply. Ms. Winmore doesn't want to start her new position with several strikes against her, and knows that Ms. Hardnose is a firm person, but a fair one. Ms. Winmore would like to move up when Ms. Hardnose retires. She also wants to make a good impression on the staff, the library board of directors, and the city's officials. What should she do? She knows that the ADA is reality and will not go away.

Gently, but firmly, she takes command of the orientation session and explains to Ms. Hardnose that the ADA requires all libraries employing 50 or more people to designate a responsible library employee to coordinate information about the ADA. Ms. Winmore then volunteers to serve as the ADA coordinator for the library. Ms. Hardnose gratefully accepts Ms. Winmore's offer and immediately appoints her the library's ADA coordinator.

Upon acceptance of this additional responsibility, Ms. Winmore explains that her designation as ADA coordinator in no way limits the library's obligation to ensure that all of its employees comply with the ADA in providing service to all library patrons, including those with disabilities.[1] Her appointment could, however, insure that any failure by individual employees in providing library service to patrons with disabilities could be promptly corrected.

## CASE 2: A FRUSTRATED RESEARCHER

Because of increasing central vision loss in both of his eyes, associated with macular degeneration, Dr. Freddie Everedi, a noted sparkplug scientist, is now temporarily medically retired. He is on long-term disability (LTD) leave from his position as chief researcher in the Quality Control Laboratory of Always Sparking Plugs, Unlimited, a private, for-profit company. Dr. Everedi has also had coronary bypass surgery and suffers from arteriosclerosis.

A voracious reader of popular fiction and nonfiction books on the occult, Dr. Everedi's immediate personal reading needs are satisfied through individual subscription service from the National Library Service for the Blind and Physically Handicapped, from which he receives talking (cassette) books almost weekly.

While Dr. Everedi retains substantial peripheral vision, his ability to read has been seriously impaired. Through the use of a magnifier, an assistive device, he has been able to slowly read his professional secondary literature, sparkplug technology. Unfortunately, the bulk of primary research materials in this area is only available in written form. Also, this very specialized material is not available on loan from the National Library Service for the Blind and Physically Handicapped.

The ADA defines Dr. Everedi as an individual with a qualified disability. His popular reading needs have been satisfied by the NLS, but what about his personal need to remain current in his vocational field of sparkplug technology? Because of the remote geographic location of the company plant, Dr. Everedi does not have immediate physical access to a public university or major public library's collection of sparkplug technology materials either in print or nonprint format. What responsibility does the Special Sparkplug Library of Always Sparking Plugs, Unlimited have in meeting Dr. Everedi's professional reading needs? Even though Dr. Everedi is on LTD leave, he technically is an employee of Always Sparking Plugs, Unlimited, and eligible to use the company's special library.

Under the ADA a private entity library, such as the Special Sparkplug Library of Always Sparking Plugs, Unlimited, is not required to actually stock accessible or special materials, such as Braille or taped books, but it must interlibrary loan these materials if desired by an eligible user, such as Dr. Everedi.[2]

If the Special Sparkplug Library was a public entity the ADA would apply, in that individuals with visual disabilities cannot benefit from the library service of book circulation unless large print, taped, and Braille reading materials are available for loan to any qualified individual who needs them. These formats are explicitly included in the U.S. Department of Justice's list of auxiliary aids and services.

It might be a continuing undue financial burden for the private Special Sparkplug Library to create sparkplug technology materials in the alternate formats of Braille, large print, or on audiotape if Dr. Everedi was the only user of these materials, and if they were not available on interlibrary loan from another library. What then is the solution to Dr. Everedi's problem? Also, what responsibility does the Special Sparkplug Library have in accommodating Dr. Everedi's need for library service?

As a possible accommodation, the library could purchase a speech synthesizer (also called voice output) for use with the library's online catalog or other electronically stored information, and for Dr. Everedi's use of print materials in the library. Also, through OCR (optical character recognition) capabilities, the information on a page can be scanned and transformed into audible information. These types of assistive devices may be available on loan to Dr. Everedi, as a qualified individual with a visual disability, from the state's governmental unit of blind services. Also, as a person with a qualified visual disability, Dr. Everedi may apply for, and receive, a grant from the state's unit of blind services to purchase a speech synthesizer and other related equipment for his personal and individual use.

Since Dr. Everedi is a noted sparkplug scientist, and his LTD leave may be considered temporary, and as an eligible user of the company's library, the best possible accommodation would be for Always Sparking Plugs, Unlimited, to purchase a speech synthesizer for Dr. Everedi's use in the Special Sparkplug Library. The costs for equipment would not be prohibitive, provided the library maintained high-tech computer equipment; the price range would be approximately $2000 to $4000. This would resolve Dr. Everedi's accommodation provided he had transportation to the company's library.

## CASE 3: THE POSTED NOTICES

The newly appointed ADA coordinator for a state library posted notices of nondiscrimination under the provisions of Title I of the ADA on the public and staff bulletin boards of the library, as prescribed by the ADA. Under ADA Section 105—Posting Notices (42 *USC* 11215)— Every employer . . . covered under Title I (Employment) shall post notices in an accessible format to applicants, employees, and members describing the applicable provisions of the ADA, in the manner prescribed by Section 711 of the Civil Rights Act of 1964—(42 *USC* 2000e-10). Almost immediately after reading the notice, the president (a wheelchair user) of the library's staff association scheduled a meeting of the association to discuss an affirmative action plan for individuals with disabilities which would apply to the library.

The state library director, the ADA coordinator, and the EEOC officer for the library were invited (by correspondence) to the scheduled staff meeting by the association's president. In the correspondence, the president listed the subject of the meeting as: *An Affirmative Action Plan for the State Library Under the Americans with Disabilities Act of 1990.* The president glanced at a copy of the ADA just prior to the scheduled meeting.

At the beginning of the meeting, as a form of introduction for the subject of the meeting, the president briefly explained Title I to the assembled group. Following this, the ADA coordinator was introduced by the president.

After the usual welcoming remarks, the ADA coordinator said: "This is an excellent opportunity for me to talk to this group about the Americans with Disabilities Act and how it will apply to the libraries in the state." After a complete explanation of the ADA, the coordinator continued, "Under the ADA's Section 502 a state is not immune under the eleventh amendment to the Constitution of the United States from an action in federal or state court of competent jurisdiction for a violation of the ADA. In any action against a state for a violation of the requirements of the ADA, remedies, including remedies both at law and in equity, are available for such a violation to the same extent as such remedies are available for such a violation in an action against any public or private entity other than a state."[3]

At this point, a member of the association said to the coordinator, "I don't understand all that doubletalk about the state. Does that mean that if the state library doesn't hire a qualified person because of a disability the state library is immune from any charges of discrimination?" In response, the coordinator said, "No, under the ADA, the state library is not immune from a charge of discrimination for not hiring a qualified person with a disability. Like any public or private entity covered by the ADA, this library cannot discriminate against a qualified person with a disability, because of the disability, in regard to job application procedures. In fact, if the person with a disability can perform the essential functions of the position, as stated in the written job description, then there cannot be any discrimination against that person, because of the disability, and, if necessary, under Section 101(9)(A), the library must make the existing work area accessible, and provide the necessary adaptive equipment to accomplish the job."

The president of the association asked, "Then this means that the state library can develop an affirmative action plan for the hiring of qualified people with disabilities, provided they can do the jobs?" The ADA coordinator replied, "There is nothing in the Americans with Disabilities Act or the regulations or guidelines that allows for, or calls for, an affirmative action plan for hiring people with disabilities to be established in the workplace; and further, the Act is not an affirmative action statute. The objective of the ADA is to eliminate employment barriers for those qualified people with disabilities." (*See* Chapter 4 for discussion of affirmative action and the ADA.)

The state library director explained: "Under our compliance with Section 504 of the Rehabilitation Act of 1973, since the state library received federal funding, it was necessary to develop an affirmative action plan to hire qualified people with disabilities. This is not the situation under the ADA."

After this, the ADA coordinator stated: "In actuality the ADA is more broad in that discrimination against people with disabilities is prohibited in every respect: employment, public services and accommodations, telecommunications, and transportation."

## CASE 4: A GENDER CHANGE

Library Assistant III Billy Gene Rego (a.k.a. Billie Jean Rego), a 10-year paraprofessional in a large academic library, has within the last year undergone a surgical sex-change. Over the 10-year period, Mr. Rego has publically displayed transvestite trends at both formal and informal library functions. He openly announced his selection as drag queen of the year by the local Alternative Life Style Club for the seventh year in a row. This fact has also appeared in the university's student newspaper. (ADA Section 508—Transvestites (42 *USC* 12208) states: "For the purpose of this Act, the term—disabled—or—disability—shall not apply to an individual solely because that individual is a transvestite.")

Throughout his 10-year tenure at the library, Mr. Rego had, on an increasing basis, worn what might be considered female apparel to work. Outwardly, Mr. Rego appeared to be a female. As part of his sex transformation, he started taking female hormones about the time he began work at the library; he also underwent breast augmentation surgery, more hormone treatments, and psychological counseling (required by the medical personnel before performing any sex-change surgery). While on leave without pay from the library, Mr. Rego traveled to London, England, for the sex-change surgery.

As part of the presurgery procedure, and before he could be accepted as a suitable candidate for this type of surgery, Mr. Rego had to submit to various medical laboratory tests administered by medical doctors. One of these tests revealed that he was born with a chromosomal abnormality; he had three X chromosomes and one Y, instead of the normal pattern of XY for males and XX for females. The sex-change (or gender-reassignment) surgery was successful.

Upon returning to the United States, Mr. Rego had his name legally changed to Billie Jean Rego. He also asked the courts to recognize him as a female through a change of his birth certificate for such things as social security retirement and benefits. The local and state courts refused to treat the post-surgery patient as a female.

Shortly after returning to work in the library, Billie Jean Rego scheduled a meeting with the library director. In the meeting, she requested use of the female-staff facilities, including the restroom. She based this request on her claim of having a disability—transsexualism. Ms. Rego described some of the minor incidents that had happened in her use of the library's public restroom for men, and also on one occasion while using the staff's male restroom, prior to, and after her sex-change surgery. In one case, someone asked to see the results of the operation.

The library director was hard pressed to grant Ms. Rego's request; ADA Section 511(b)—Definitions—did not include transsexual or gender identity disorders not resulting from physical impairment under the definition for disability.[4] As an accommodation to Ms. Rego's request, the library director indicated that since all of the library staff knew of the sex-change surgery, a sign "IN USE" would be constructed for use by Ms. Rego. The sign was to be hung on the male-staff restroom door when Ms. Rego was using that facility (since confidentiality was not an issue, the staff members were to be notified of this action, on an individual basis, in private, through conferences with their respective supervisors). The library director requested that Ms. Rego restrict her use to the male-staff restroom, and avoid use of the library's public restroom for men, when, and if possible, during her working hours.

## CASE 5: THE TRANSFER

The head librarian of the school library media center, Nany Mae ReFronance, learned that the library's maintenance person, Jammi Golitle, had been staring at the students while loudly smacking her lips and hitting herself on her ears, one side at a time; she looked like she was going to fall over. Ms. ReFronance at first ignored these seemingly silly accusations about Ms. Golitle's strange behavior, but they continued and soon came to the attention of the school's principal, Jazbo Head-Coacher. Mr. Head-Coacher requested a meeting with Ms. ReFronance to discuss the alleged strange behavior of Ms. Golitle in the library in front of the students.

Before her meeting with the principal, Ms. ReFronance had a meeting with Ms. Golitle. After some friendly preliminary conversation, Ms. ReFronance asked Ms. Golitle how she had been feeling lately? Ms. Golitle replied, "I'm doing fine, except lately I've had a few headaches and stomachaches, but, outside of that, I'm feeling fine!"

She followed this by saying, "I've been getting madder and madder at my son John, I'm afraid he's going to flunk out of high school." Ms. ReFronance asked Ms. Golitle if she had seen the school's doctor or nurse about her headaches and stomachaches. Ms. Golitle indicated that she hadn't, but if Ms. ReFronance thought it was a good idea she would do so next week.

At her meeting with the principal, Ms. ReFronance said that she had met with Ms. Golitle. She told the principal about Ms. Golitle's recent headaches and stomachaches and about Ms. Golitle's worries that her son could flunk out of high school.

Ms. ReFronance told Mr. Head-Coacher that she thought it was strange that Ms. Golitle should worry about her son's academic work, because, as far as she knew, John was a straight "A" student. And, if he was having any disciplinary problems, she certainly would have heard about it "just from the school district gossip-mongers alone." Ms. ReFronance told Mr. Head-Coacher that Ms. Golitle had scheduled an appointment "for next week" with the school doctor in the school infirmary.

Written school district policy stated that if an employee of the district had what was considered a serious health problem, the principle would be notified of it after the patient (employee) had been notified. This written policy was the same for students who brought their health problems to the school's doctor or nurse, although, in such cases, the student's parents were notified before the principal.

About a week after Ms. Golitle's appointment in the school's infirmary, the school doctor called the principal and informed him that she suspected Ms. Golitle had epilepsy. She said, "I'm not completely sure, but after all of the medical laboratory tests are run we should know." Mr. Head-Coacher asked about Ms. Golitle's alleged staring, lip smacking, and hitting herself on the ears. The doctor thanked him and said, "I'll get back with you about this."

The school doctor called her colleague, a specialist in neurology, Dr. Mari Briteone, about Ms. Golitle's medical symptoms and the possibility of epilepsy. She also told Dr. Briteone about her conversation with the principal and his comments about Ms. Golitle's behavior. Dr. Briteone said, "Yes, I believe you are right about the epilepsy; the results of her medical laboratory tests seem to confirm this. The staring, lip smacking, and hitting herself on her ears, lead me to believe that she is experiencing epileptic complex partial seizures. People with epileptic complex partial seizures have periods of automatic behavior and clouded consciousness, including staring, lip smacking, headaches and stomachaches, buzzing or ringing in the ears, dizziness, or feelings of strong emotions, such as fear or rage. Also, there is no memory of these actions once the person is fully conscious again."

Upon learning of the epilepsy diagnosis, and the unconscious behavior that accompanied complex partial seizures, Ms. Golitle requested a transfer into the vacant maintenance-person position in the school's supplyroom. She felt that even if her epileptic seizures could be controlled by medication, she wanted to be in a less public area, and the supplyroom was semiprivate during most of the school day. Ms. Golitle's request for transfer was approved.

Since the head librarian did not wish to make Ms. Golitle's illness public, she announced her transfer to the supplyroom in the school library media center's *Newsletter* as a promotion for her "many years of dedicated service to the school library media center and to the school." Further, since Ms. ReFronance felt that the students didn't understand certain illnesses that caused a person to be developmentally disabled, she asked the science teacher to devote a class period to this subject and to include epilepsy. Ms. ReFronance supported her request by compiling an annotated bibliography on the subject, accompanied by a display of books and a bulletin board exhibit entitled "Epilepsy and Its Control."

After thinking about her transfer, Ms. Golitle asked the head librarian if she could have stayed in her position in the school library media center after being diagnosed as epileptic. Ms. ReFronance stated that epilepsy as a developmental disability was included under the Rehabilitation, Comprehensive Services and Developmental Disabilities Amendments of 1978, Public Law 95-502. "You are protected under the ADA because of your recognized disability and therefore it is the responsibility of the school to accommodate your needs," said Ms. ReFronance. "Since the vacant position existed, we could transfer you as you requested, but we could not have created a new position because of your disability."

Ms. ReFronance stated, "Under the ADA's Title I which is covered by Section 101(9) (b) called 'Reasonable Accommodation,' the school could reassign you to a vacant position or make another similar accommodation for your epilepsy. Since you volunteered to visit the school infirmary, this is covered under the ADA's Section 102(c)(4)(B) which is called 'Acceptable Examination and Inquires'; it allowed the school to conduct a voluntary medical examination as part of your health program available here at your worksite."[5]

## CASE 6: A REASSIGNMENT

Under the city's medical-leave policy, Jim Nowork entered the city hospital for pneumonia. He was off work for several weeks due to his hospitalization. Upon returning to work in the city public library's snackbar and cafeteria, which is open to the public, he scheduled an appointment with his supervisor and told him that he had tested positive for the Human Immunodeficiency Virus.

Mr. Nowork's supervisor wants to reassign him to another position where he will not be in contact with food. Mr. Nowork claims that this is not necessary and his supervisor agrees to look into the matter before taking any action. Mr. Nowork's position, Food Handler II, is part of the city's Civil Service Commission which regulates employment procedures for the city.

The supervisor was referred to several city departments, but could get no answer to his question: "May I transfer an employee who has tested HIV-Positive to another position within the library's Food Services Department?" He finally contacted the head of the city Public Health Department, Dr. I.M. Smart.

The personnel in the Public Health Department (PHD) said that Dr. Smart was in Paris attending an International Congress on AIDS, where he was presenting a paper on AIDS in the workplace. One of the staff members of the PHD suggested the supervisor call the state's AIDS Hotline—1 (800) 000-AIDS. After repeated busy signals, he finally got through, and was told by a volunteer to call the state's Commission on Human Services at another 800 number. A staff member at the Commission gave the supervisor yet another 800 number to call for the EEOC.

Time was a consideration, as far as the supervisor was concerned, so he called the U.S. Department of Health and Human Services, where after being left on hold for 20 minutes, he was disconnected. He then remembered something about a communicable disease center being located somewhere, so he called the long distance operator and asked for the number, finally receiving a number for a Center for Disease Control (CDC).

After reaching the CDC Library, he asked the librarian his question. The librarian replied, "Sir, I can't answer that question, but we have a series of pamphlets on AIDS that I can send you!" The supervisor thanked the librarian, but said, "No, thank you, I need a specific legal answer to my question." The librarian then said, "You should call the U.S. Department of Justice about legal questions. Have you called your city's legal counsel or your personnel department about this?"

When the supervisor was about to give up and forget the whole issue, Dr. Smart telephoned him and addressed his question. The supervisor learned from Dr. Smart that HIV infection is not transmitted through food; is a covered disability under the ADA; and does not create a direct health threat to others when a person infected with HIV works as a foodhandler.

Dr. Smart told the supervisor that the Centers for Disease Control were in the U.S. Public Health Service of the U.S. Department of Health and Human Services, and that the Secretary of that department had published a *List of Infectious and Communicable Diseases That Are Transmitted Through Handling of Food Supply*. According to Dr. Smart, this was required under Section 103 (d) of the ADA."[6] The supervisor learned that HIV disease, symptomatic or asymptomatic, and AIDS were not mentioned on the *List*. Dr. Smart further stated, "in Section 35.104 of the regulation for the ADA's Subtitle A of Title II for public services, HIV disease is a covered disability. Also, under the EEOC-prepared regulations for ADA's Title I for employment, HIV infections are considered inherently substantially limiting and as such, a physical impairment exists.[7]"

The supervisor of the Food Services Department, formerly bent on the reassignment of Mr. Nowork to another position was forced to change his mind. Mr. Nowork was able to retain his position as a Food Handler II in the city library's snackbar and cafeteria. The supervisor knew that his decision would affect other libraries that had snackbars and cafeterias which were open to the public.

## THE ADA LIBRARY COMMITTEE—AN EXERCISE

What follows is a sample memorandum from a director of a large county library to the library staff. The library has 192 full-time employees, 150 part-time employees, 100-200 volunteers, and 1 central library, 27 branch libraries, and 4 bookmobiles. A subregional talking-book library serving four counties is located in the central library building, and each branch library and bookmobile has a deposit collection of blind and physically handicapped materials and equipment. All libraries in the county meet architectural guidelines, and are fully accessible to people with disabilities.

When you read the following memorandum, imagine you are the county library director. Based on the description of the county library above do you think you would have any difficulty 1) forming an effective staff-patron ADA library committee, 2) complying with the regulations and guidelines of the ADA, and 3) meeting the compliance deadlines of the ADA?

After you have read the memorandum, answer the questions that follow with your library (materials and equipment, staff, facilities, services, resources, programs, policies and procedures, etc.) in mind. Are you personally ready for the ADA?

---

### Memorandum

DATE:      Any date
TO:        All County Library Staff
FROM:      Director of Libraries
SUBJECT:   Americans with Disabilities Act (ADA) Library Committee

The Americans with Disabilities Act (ADA), signed into law by President Bush, promises to provide comprehensive civil rights protection to individuals with disabilities in the areas of employment, state and local government services, public accommodations, and telecommunications. Titles I, II, and III of this law apply to libraries, and compliance is required by July 1992 for employment, and January 26, 1992, for programs and services and physical accessibility.

In order to meet the requirements of this new law and to find appropriate ways to make the County Library System's programs and services accessible to all people with disabilities, I would like to form a committee to develop a proposed plan of action. The committee will study the requirements of the ADA and the federal regulations; and, with input from library patrons with disabilities, make suggestions to me as to the best way to carry out both the letter and the spirit of this legislation.

If you would like to be on the CL-ADA Library Committee, please call my office indicating your interest in serving. I would like a broad spectrum of members since the ADA will affect all aspects of library services, including employment. I will appoint the committee the following week. The first meeting will be scheduled shortly thereafter.

---

## Questions

Who on your library staff would be responsible enough, and caring enough, to serve as the ADA coordinator for your library?

Do you believe there are members on your library staff who would be willing to serve on an ADA library committee for your library?

What would you do to solicit patrons with disabilities to volunteer to serve on the ADA library committee?

How would you ensure that you had a representative group of people with disabilities serving on your ADA library committee?

Would you appoint a member of your library community to committee membership if the person was not a registered library borrower? What if this person who volunteered had a qualified disability?

Are you aware of the physical condition of the libraries in your system? Will these libraries qualify architecturally under the ADA regulations?

If you have a library board, what would they think about the ADA? How would you go about providing orientation sessions on the ADA for the library board? The staff? Your patrons?

Would your administrative entity provide you with any financial or other assistance in meeting the employment, public services, and architectural regulations and guidelines under the ADA?

Are you aware of what type of service is available from your state's regional library for the blind and physically handicapped?

What type of support assistance can you expect from your state agency? Does it provide ADA consultants?

## ADA QUESTIONS AND ANSWERS—AN EXERCISE

The case studies should have provided enough information to readers to allow them to see that it is just a matter of knowing and applying the ADA, its rules and regulations, and its guidelines in order to provide equal opportunity for individuals with disabilities in employment, public services, public accommodations, and telecommunications in their libraries.

Below are a series of questions that can be answered by using the Americans with Disabilities Act itself, or by using the ADA rules and regulations. The answers given here can help guide you in confronting similar questions and problems in your workplace by using the ADA regulations and guidelines.

## Questions and Answers

**Question:** If my library system operates bookmobile service, is this covered under the ADA?

**Answer:** Bookmobiles or related activities are covered by the requirement for program accessibility in §35.150 and would be included in the ADA definition of a facility like other real property, although standards for new construction and alterations are not yet included in the accessibility standards adopted by §35.151 of the ADA regulations (56 *Federal Register* 35708-35711).

**Question:** Are TDDs required in each external extension of a library system, such as a branch library?

**Answer:** The Department of Justice encourages those entities that have extensive telephone contact with the public, such as public libraries, to have TDDs (Telecommunication Devices for the Deaf) to ensure more immediate access. Where the provision of telephone service is a major function of the entity, such as a business reference section in a major city library, or Information and Referral services, TDDs should be available. This is covered in the ADA regulations in §35.161—Telecommunication Devices for the Deaf (TDD) (56 *Federal Register* 35712).

**Question:** If your library completed a self-evaluation under Section 504 of the Rehabilitation Act of 1973, is it necessary to do another self-evaluation under the ADA?

**Answer:** The ADA Regulation in §35.105 (Self-evaluation) established a requirement, based on Section 504 regulations of the Rehabilitation Act of 1973, that a public entity, for federally assisted and federally conducted programs, evaluate its current policies and practices to identify and correct any that are not consistent with the requirements of the ADA (56 *Federal Register* 35701).

**Question:** Does coverage of people with contagious diseases mean that such people can never be excluded from a job?

**Answer:** The ADA regulation for Title I (Employment) in §1630.2(r) (Direct Threat) reads: "An employer may require, as a qualification standard, that an individual not pose a direct threat to the health or safety of himself/herself or others. Like any other qualification standard, such a standard must apply to all applicants or employees and not just to individuals with disabilities. If, however, an individual poses a direct threat as a result of the disability, the employer must determine whether a reasonable accommodation would either eliminate the risk or reduce it to acceptable level. If no accommodation exists that would either eliminate or reduce the risk, the employer may refuse to hire an applicant or may discharge an employee who poses a direct threat" (56 *Federal Register* 35745).

**Question:** If your library's community room or auditorium is used by a professional association to offer courses and examinations leading to certification and/or licensing, are there any specific restrictions placed on these activities under the ADA?

**Answer:** ADA Title III (Public Accommodations . . .) in §309 (Examinations and Courses) reads: "Any person that offers examinations, or credentialing for secondary or postsecondary education, professional or trade purposes shall offer such examinations or courses in a place and manner accessible to persons with disabilities or offer alternative arrangements for such individuals (42 *USC* 12189). (This one was answered in the Act.)

**Question:** Is a church library covered under the ADA?

**Answer:** In the ADA Title III (Public Accommodations . . .) in §307 (Exemptions For . . . and Religious Organizations) reads: "The provision of this title (Title III) shall not apply to . . . establishments exempted under Title II of the Civil Rights Act of 1964 or to religious organizations or entities controlled by religious organizations . . . ." (42 *USC* 12187). (Another one answered in the Act.)

Religious organizations may require that all applicants and employees conform to the religious tenets of the church (ADA Section 103 (c) (2). These organizations may not discriminate against an individual who satisfies the religious criteria because that individual is disabled (56 *Federal Register* 35752).

**Question:**  Does the ADA require an affirmative action plan? Does it require goals, timetables, and quotas?

**Answer:**  Nowhere in the ADA or the rules and regulations or the guidelines is there a provision made for an affirmative action plan. There are timetables for compliance to the various sections of the titles in the ADA. (See Appendix B, "Americans with Disabilities Act Statutory Deadlines.") There are no provisions in the ADA for quotas.

## ACTION ON THE ADA BY ANY STATE LIBRARY AGENCY— A RECOMMENDATION

Below is an example of the type of cooperative implementation of the Americans with Disabilities Act of 1990 in libraries (in this case, public libraries) that could be followed in any state, by any state library agency. If librarians (directors/administrators/managers) are to be effective in their individual efforts, it would be extremely beneficial if their respective state library agencies would take the lead by coordinating and guiding these activities through a statewide effort.

---

**Any State Library Agency—Memorandum**

TO:    Library Directors
FROM: State Librarian
DATE:  Any Date
RE:      Americans with Disabilities Act (ADA) of 1990

The Americans with Disabilities Act (ADA) of 1990 is new federal legislation that applies to all public services and accommodations, including both publicly and privately funded libraries. The following materials are enclosed for your information and to assist you in determining the implications of this legislation for your library:

A copy of the Americans with Disabilities Act (ADA) of 1990

Brief summaries of the law and the statutory deadlines

Information on the federal regulations developed to guide the administration of the law

A bibliography of publications about the ADA

A list of suggestions to assist libraries in implementing the law

The materials include the implementation dates for the various titles of the Act. In particular, Title II, Public Services, is scheduled to go into effect on January 26, 1992.

The state library agency has established a Task Force on Accessibility, a group of librarians and consumers, to advise this agency on ways to keep the library community informed about this new law. Future plans include information documents, training activities, and updates in the agency's publication. Your governing agency or administration may also be providing information to you on responding to the requirements of the legislation.

---

**Implementing the ADA—Planning Suggestions from the State Library Agency**

1.  This legislation has an impact on every area of library service: employment, materials and equipment, physical plant, etc. As libraries review and plan in the regular process for developing their programs of

service, they will want to consciously include the step of assuring that services and facilities presently available, and those planned for the future, are equally available to all citizens. Developing a comprehensive approach that includes considering the requirements of this new law as part of the total planning process is recommended.

2. Libraries can start now to recruit individuals with disabilities and integrate their organizations. Managers should identify the essential job functions of various positions and list those in each job description, as the test of whether or not an individual can do a job revolves around his or her ability to do identified essential job functions.

3. Planning groups to assess and develop ADA implementation efforts can be assembled now. These groups should include consumers who have disabilities, as the law requires that users of a service be consulted concerning their needs.

4. The planning group can begin the process of assessing your existing employment opportunities, library services, materials, and physical plan access. Beginning this work now will allow you to include needed items in your next budget request.

5. The ADA will affect all the components of public service agencies, not just the library. Contacting your governing agency or board now will allow you to provide information about the ADA and to participate in agencywide planning.

## CLOSURE

Critics might wish to chastise the authors of this chapter for their seemingly flippant name selection for their cast in the case studies, such as Mr. Nowork and Ms. Golitle. This was done because the authors wished to lighten or add some nonjudicious levity to a very serious subject—providing equal library service to individuals with disabilities.

In selecting types of disabilities or nondisabilities in the case studies, the authors attempted to select those that might be considered borderline and possibly controversial, such as being tested HIV-Positive. This issue is receiving more and more national attention. On November 7, 1991, Earvin "Magic" Johnson, the internationally known basketball great of the Los Angles Lakers publically announced that he had tested positive for the HIV virus. In doing so, he also announced his resignation from the Lakers and from professional basketball. Following this public announcement, every major national television network carried a special on Johnson and the HIV virus. Stories appeared in every type of printed news media, and not just in the sports section but on the front page. Safe sex became a major issue for classroom discussion in schools throughout the nation, and, most likely, throughout the world. Before this, HIV apparently was only a major issue in food service and medical-dental institutions.

When we think of disabilities, we need to consider individuals with hidden disabilities, such as children born with drug addiction because their mothers were addicted to drugs. Individuals suffering with coronary diseases must prove their disabilities through certification by a medical doctor. Until such certification is obtained the individual may be disabled, but it may not seem outwardly limiting in a major life activity to those observing his or her activities.

In "Case 2: A Frustrated Researcher," the authors gave Dr. Freddie Everedi a vision loss due to macular degeneration, which may or may not have been caused by Dr. Everedi's arteriosclerosis. Vision loss in most forms limits some of the major life activities, such as "caring for one's self and walking." Cardiovascular disease is also a covered disability and affects several of life's major activities, "performing manual tasks, breathing, and working." In a sense, Dr. Everedi had two covered disabilities, a cardiovascular disease and vision loss.

Even though vision loss is a covered disability, in order to receive service from a National Library Service for the Blind and Physically Handicapped network library, the person with the vision loss has to be certified as to his or her level of loss. Many people who seem to be without disabilities could probably qualify for covered disability status; Test A in an ADA rule on disabilities reads: ". . . when the individual's important life activities are restricted as to the conditions, manner or duration under which they can be performed in comparison to most people" (*Source:* ADA Rule for Title III—Test A §36.104—56 *Federal Register* 35549).

There could have been a case study describing an older person, male or female, who used a wheelchair and sought access to a public library. After many difficulties, the person got up and walked into the library without assistance. Upon investigation, it is discovered that the library patron didn't need the wheelchair, but because of his or her advancing age used one for greater mobility. In visiting over 200 nursing homes, the authors found that it was almost standard practice for each resident of a nursing facility to have his or her own wheelchair to expedite mobility, even if the person didn't medically need one. Aging may some day be a covered disability. Now it has to be associated with another condition, medical or otherwise. The case studies constructed here were to highlight the ADA and its rules and regulations and guidelines, not the disability in its treatment.

The authors of this chapter are fully responsible for the interpretations of the ADA and its various rules and regulations. They also are responsible for the construction of the case studies. This is not meant to claim credit, but to lay blame (if needed) for any misinterpretations or misconceptions in this chapter. This too applies for the other chapter contributors.

## REFERENCES

1. 56 *Federal Register* 35702.
2. 56 *Federal Register* 35598.
3. 42 *USC* 12202.
4. 42 *USC* 12111.
5. 42 *USC* 12112.
6. 56 *Federal Register* 22726-22727.
7. 56 *Federal Register* 35741.

## CHAPTER 6

# Problem Areas and a Quick Guide to the ADA

### DONALD D. FOOS AND NANCY C. PACK

### PROBLEMATIC AREAS IN THE ADA

Case study material abounds in the rule that governs Title II (Public Services) of the Americans with Disabilities Act. For example, those municipalities that still have operational historic Carnegie Libraries (especially those on the National Register of Historic Places) will have difficulties in the possible restructuring of these buildings to comply under the physical accessibility clauses in the ADA rule. But, these items (not the Carnegie Libraries per se) are included in the rule. Similar problems might exist for those public library systems that lease facilities, such as older, former store-front buildings, or in malls. These might also have difficulties in providing physical access to their services and programs. But, then again, these leased types of facilities are included in the ADA rule.

The items in this section have been selected for their problematic nature. The rule that implements Subtitle A of Title II (Public Services) of the ADA, which prohibits discrimination on the basis of disability by public entities, was utilized for this purpose. Public Services were selected because providing services, programs, and resources to their respective service areas is what libraries are all about.

The U.S. Department of Justice's Rule (28 *CFR* Part 35) on Nondiscrimination on the Basis of Disability in State and Local Government Services; Final Rule, as published in the *Federal Register* for July 26, 1991 (56 *Federal Register* 35694-35723) was referenced in this section. This Final Rule (28 *CFR* Part 35) is available from the U.S.

Department of Justice. Case studies could have been developed on any one of the items listed below. They were selected to show the reader what is covered in the rule governing Title II (Public Services). They are in alphabetical order and are not ranked by importance.

**ADA Coordinator**—The designation of an employee responsible for the coordination of efforts to carry out responsibilities under Title II must in no way limit a public entity's obligation to ensure that all of its employees comply with the requirements of the rule. It ensures that any failure by individual employees can be promptly corrected by the designated employee, the ADA coordinator (56 *Federal Register* 35702).

**Attendants**—Public entities may not require that a qualified individual with a disability be accompanied by an attendant. A public entity is not required to provide attendant care, or assistance, such as in toileting, etc., to individuals with disabilities (56 *Federal Register* 35705).

**Auxiliary Aids**—The public entity must provide an opportunity for individuals with disabilities to request the auxiliary aids and services of their choice. This expressed choice will be given primary consideration by the public entity. The public entity will honor the choice unless it can demonstrate that another effective means of communication exists or that use of the means chosen "would not be required under §35.164" (56 *Federal Register* 35712).

**Carrying**—Carrying an individual with a disability is considered an ineffective and unacceptable method of achieving program accessibility (56 *Federal Register* 35709).

**Complaints**—If two or more agencies have apparent responsibility over a complaint, the U.S. Assistant Attorney General shall be the designated agency for purposes of the compliant (56 *Federal Register* 35723).

**Disability**—The use of the term "disability" instead of "handicap" and the term "individual with a disability" instead of "individuals with handicaps" represents an effort by the U.S. Congress to make use of up-to-date currently accepted terminology. For instance, the National Council on the Handicapped is now the National Council on Disability (Public Law 100-630) (56 *Federal Register* 35698).

**Government Documents**—Reading devices or readers should be provided when necessary for equal participation and opportunity to benefit from any governmental service, program, or activity, such as reviewing public documents (56 *Federal Register* 35712).

**Historic Preservation**—Where historic preservation is not the primary purpose of the program, the public entity is not required to use a particular facility. It can relocate all or part of its program to an accessible facility, make home visits, or use other standard methods of achieving program accessibility without making structural alternations that might threaten or destroy the significant historic features of the historic property. Thus, programs in historic properties are not excused from the requirement for program access (See also National Register) (56 *Federal Register* 35709).

**HIV**—In the definition of disability it was concluded that asymptomatic HIV disease is an impairment that substantially limits a major life activity, either because of its actual effect on the individual with HIV disease or because the reactions of other people to individuals with the HIV disease cause such individuals to be treated as though they were disabled (56 *Federal Register* 35698).

**Home Visits**—The public entity may comply with the program accessibility requirement by delivering services at alternate sites or making home visits as appropriate (56 *Federal Register* 35709).

**Integration**—Integration is fundamental to the purpose of the ADA. The provision of segregated accommodations and services relegates persons with disabilities to second-class status. For example, it would be a violation of this provision to require persons with disabilities to eat in the back of the library's cafeteria or to refuse to allow a person with a disability the full use of a facility because of stereotypes about the person's ability to participate. Modified participation for persons with disabilities must be a choice of the person not a requirement (56 *Federal Register* 35703).

**Law Enforcement**—The general regulatory obligation to modify policies, practices, or procedures requires law enforcement to make changes in policies that result in discriminatory arrests or abuse of individuals with disabilities. Law enforcement personnel are required to make appropriate efforts to determine whether perceived strange or disruptive behavior (such as a library patron diagnosed as having Tourett's syndrome) or unconsciousness is a result of a disability (See "ADAPT and the ADA" below) (56 *Federal Register* 35703).

**Leased Buildings**—Existing buildings leased by public entities after the effective date of Final Rule (28 *CFR* Part 35) are not required by the regulation to meet accessibility standards simply by the virtue of being leased. They are subject to the program accessibility standard for existing facilities. Requiring that public entities only lease accessible space would significantly restrict the options of state and local governments in seeking leased space, which would be particularly burdensome in rural or sparsely populated areas. Requirements are not applicable to buildings leased by public entities. They are encouraged to look for the most accessible space available to lease and to attempt to find space complying at least with minimum federal requirements (56 *Federal Register* 35711).

**Library Registration**—Requiring the presentation of a driver's license as the sole means of identification would violate the intent of the ADA in situations where, for example, individuals with severe vision impairments or developmental disabilities or epilepsy are ineligible to receive a driver's license and the use of an alternative means of identification, such as another photo ID or credit card, is feasible (56 *Federal Register* 35705).

**Myths**—The U.S. Congress acknowledged that society's accumulated myths and fears about disability and disease are as handicapping as are the physical limitations that flow from actual impairment. Thus, a person who is denied services or benefits by a public entity because of myths, fears, and stereotypes associated with disabilities is covered under the ADA regulations (56 *Federal Register* 35700).

**National Register**—A definition of "historic property" drawn from Section 504 (Sites Eligible for Listing in National Register) of the ADA has been added to clarify that the term applies to those properties listed or eligible for listing in the National Register of Historic Places, or properties designated as historic under state or local laws. If it has been determined under the procedures established that it is not feasible to provide physical access to an historic property in a manner that will not threaten or destroy the historic significance of the property, alternative methods of access will be provided in accordance with the requirements for public access (56 *Federal Register* 35711).

**Qualified Interpreter**—In order to clarify what was meant in the statute by "qualified interpreter"—the U.S. Department of Justice added a definition of the term to the final rule. A qualified interpreter means an interpreter who is able to interpret effectively, accurately, and expressively, using any specialized vocabulary, such as in medicine. This definition focuses on the actual ability of the interpreter in a particular interpreting context to facilitate effective communication between the public entity and the individuals with disabilities (56 *Federal Register* 35701).

**Readily Achievable**—Title II of the ADA requires a public entity to make its programs accessible in all cases, except where it would result in a fundamental alteration in the nature of the program or in undue financial and administrative burdens. The program access requirement of Title II should enable individuals with disabilities to participate in and benefit from the services, programs, or activities of public entities in all but the most unusual cases (56 *Federal Register* 35708).

**Screening-out**—The ADA rule prohibits the imposition or application of eligibility criteria that screen-out or tend to screen-out an individual with a disability or any class or individuals with disabilities from fully and equally enjoying any service, program, or activity, unless such criteria can be shown to be necessary for the provision of the service, program, or activity being offered (56 *Federal Register* 35704).

**Smoking**—The Act does not preclude the prohibition of, or imposition of, restrictions on smoking in transportation covered in Title II. Commenters on the Act argued that this section was too limited in scope, and that the regulations would prohibit smoking in all facilities used by public entities. The reference to smoking in Section 501 merely clarifies the Act and does not require public entities to accommodate smoking by permitting smoking in [public] facilities (56 *Federal Register* 35707).

**Surcharge**—A public entity may not place a surcharge on a particular individual with a disability, or any group of individuals with disabilities, to cover any costs of measures required to provide that individual or group with nondiscriminatory treatment required by the Act or the Final Rule, Part 35 (56 *Federal Register* 35705).

**TDDs**—The U.S. Department of Justice was asked to replace the term "Telecommunication Devices for Deaf persons" or "TDDs" with the term "text telephones." The U.S. Department of Justice declined to do so, although aware that the U.S. Architectural and Transport Barriers Compliance Board used the phrase "text telephone" in lieu of the statutory term "TDD" in its final accessibility guidelines. Title

IV of the ADA used the term "Telecommunications Device for the Deaf" and the U.S. Department of Justice believed it was inappropriate to abandon this statutory term at that time (56 *Federal Register* 35697).

**Training**—Commenters on the ADA rule for Title II, suggested that the rule should require every self-evaluation to include an examination of training efforts to assure that individuals with disabilities were not subjected to discrimination because of insensitivity, particularly in the law enforcement area (such as library guards in major city libraries). The U.S. Department of Justice did not add such a specific requirement to the rule. It would be appropriate for public entities to evaluate training efforts because, in many cases, lack of training leads to discriminatory practices, even when the policies are nondiscriminatory (56 *Federal Register* 35702).

## A QUICK GUIDE—ADA FINAL REGULATIONS

### Title II (Public Services)

This quick guide was developed to highlight the important points in the Americans with Disabilities Act (ADA) of 1990 and its regulations that relate to Title II (Public Services). The lead-in for each entry has the subject of the section, followed by a brief explanation of the important aspects of the section. The page citation is given in parentheses.

**Policies and Practices**—Section 35.105 (56 *Federal Register* 35701-35702) of the regulation requires that all public entities (libraries) evaluate current policies and practices to identify and correct any that are not consistent with the requirements of the regulations. This activity is referred to as a self-evaluation. Any entity (library) that conducted a self-evaluation because of a similar requirement of the Rehabilitation Act of 1973 must evaluate only those areas of service or policy that were not reviewed in the previous self-evaluation. However, the regulations recommend that public entities (libraries) reexamine all of their policies and programs because of the length of time since a previous self-evaluation would have been conducted and the differences in the requirements between the Rehabilitation Act of 1973 and the ADA.

For entities (libraries) that employ 50 or more people, the self-evaluation must be kept on file at least three years. Entities (libraries) have a year to conduct the self-evaluation, but are not protected from discrimination claims during the year. The regulation also indicates that it is essential to seek the assistance of individuals with disabilities in the self-evaluation and planning for compliance process.

**Dissemination of Information**—Section 35.106 (56 *Federal Register* 35702) of the regulation requires that a public entity (library) disseminate sufficient information to applicants, participants, beneficiaries, and other interested persons to inform them of the rights and protections by the ADA and the regulations. A number of methods for providing this notice are suggested: handbooks, manuals, pamphlets, information posters, radio, and/or television. Such notice must be provided in the formats that are accessible to consumers (patrons of the library) with disabilities.

**Responsible Employee**—Section 35.107 (56 *Federal Register* 35702) of the regulation requires that entities (libraries) employing 50 or more people (staff) must designate a responsible employee (staff member) to coordinate information about the ADA. The name, telephone number, and office address of this person or persons must be made available to all interested individuals (staff members, patrons of the library, etc.).

**Grievance Procedures**—Section 35.107 (56 *Federal Register* 35702) of the regulation requires that public entities (libraries) with 50 or more employees (staff) adopt grievance procedures for resolving complaints or violations of the regulations.

**Source**: State Library of Florida, Florida Department of State, *Orange Seed— Technical Bulletin* (July-October 1991)19:Nos. 4&5:1-2.

**Note**: For purposes of this publication, entities are libraries—academic, public, school, and special.

# REHABILITATION ACT OF 1973

## Section 504

Throughout this book, references are repeatedly made to Section 504 of the Rehabilitation Act of 1973, as it relates to, or is compared to, the Americans with Disabilities Act. Therefore, this section has been prepared to provide information on Section 504 and how it has impacted libraries over the past 19 years. Unless, in quotes, *handicapped* will be replaced by *people or individual(s)* or *person(s) with disability(ies)* the current term is recommended. Further information on Section 504 can be located in: U.S. President's Committee on Employment of the Handicapped, *A Librarians Guide to 504: A Pocket Guide* (Washington, DC:GPO,1979).

**What is Section 504?**—Libraries, and every institution receiving federal funds, must take steps to insure people with disabilities are included as participants or beneficiaries of programs, resources, and services they offer. Section 504 reads: "No otherwise handicapped individual in the United States . . . shall solely by reason of his [or her] handicap, be excluded from the participation in, be denied the benefits of, or be subjected to discrimination under any program or activity receiving Federal financial assistance."

**Assurance of Nondiscrimination**—Only state libraries are required to file an assurance of compliance. State libraries are expected to monitor the compliance efforts on the local level.

**People with Disabilities**—The regulations governing Section 504 indicate that a person with a disability is anyone who: 1) has a physical or mental impairment which substantially limits one or more of the person's major life activities, 2) has a record of such impairment, and 3) is regarded as having such as impairment. The term disability includes orthopedic disorders, mental retardation, mental illness, speech and hearing disorders, perceptual dysfunction, visual impairment, specific learning disabilities, and other diseases and conditions.

**Alcoholics and Drug Addicts**—Under Section 504, in accordance with a formal opinion rendered by the U.S. Attorney General, "alcoholics and drug addicts are also considered as handicapped persons and eligible for protection of Section 504 as long as the use of alcohol or drugs does not prevent them from doing their job." Section 104(a) of the ADA reads: "for purposes of its title [Title I—Employment] the term 'qualified individual with a disability' shall not include any employee or applicant who is currently engaging in the illegal use of drugs, when the covered entity acts on the basis of such use" (42 *USC* 11214). ADA Section 104 (b) reads: "Nothing in Subsection (a) shall be construed to exclude as a qualified individual with a disability an individual who—(1) has successfully completed a supervised rehabilitation program . . . (2) is participating in a supervised rehabilitation program and no longer engaging in such use" (42 *USC* 11214). Concerning alcoholics, ADA Section 104(c)(4) reads: "may hold an employee . . . who is an alcoholic to the same qualification standards for employment or job performance and behavior that such entity holds other employees, even if any unsatisfactory performance or behavior is related to the drug use or alcoholism of such employees . . . " (42 *USC* 12114).

**Major Life Activities**—These include communication, ambulation, self-care, the ability to read, education, transportation, employment, and other things.

**Program Accessibility**—This means that programs, resources, and services offered by a library or any recipient of federal funds must be accessible through some means. This does not require every building in the system to be accessible as long as the programs, resources, and services are.

**Structural Changes**—Structural changes are not necessary if you can make programs, resources, and services accessible to persons with disabilities by moving them from an inaccessible to an accessible place. The former U.S. Department of Health, Education and Welfare issued a policy interpretation which gave small facilities, including small or rural libraries, flexibility in the way they achieved compliance with the Section 504 requirement that programs be accessible to people with disabilities. The interpretation said, in part, mobility impaired persons may be provided access to the library's services through a bookmobile, or by special messenger service, or clerical aid, or any other methods that make the resources of the library readily accessible.

**Warning**—In meeting the objective of program accessibility, you must be careful not to isolate, segregate, or concentrate handicapped individuals in settings away from nonhandicapped persons.

**Academic and School Libraries**—Materials held by libraries in educational institutions must be made available to handicapped people, if they are required for the educational process. This may mean providing the material in an alternate format. Absence of auxiliary aids for people with impaired manual, sensory, or speaking skills is no excuse for not providing material.

**Print Material**—If any library provides print material to a student, it must also provide the same material in an alternate format to a handicapped student, unable to read conventional ink print, if a request is made by the student or the instructor.

**Confidentiality**—Handicapped people do not have to step forward. Refusal to do so cannot be used against them. If handicapped people do provide information about their conditions the information must be kept confidential. An exception is to inform work supervisors if restructuring or accommodations are needed; and first-aid people may be informed of conditions so that they'll know what to do in an emergency.

## ADAPT AND THE ADA

The forceful activities of the militant disability-rights advocacy group ADAPT (Americans Disabled for Attendant Persons Today) illustrate the effectiveness of a militant advocacy group, and serve as an excellent study of human dynamics in action.

After Congress passed the Americans with Disabilities Act, which required that all new buses be equipped with hydraulic lifts, the Denver-based group called ADAPT (formerly the Americans Disabled for Accessible Public Transportation) began protesting for federal subsidies (from MEDICAID) for personal attendants, individuals hired by those with physical disabilities to help them with basic everyday needs. ADAPT wants 25% of the more than $20 billion paid to nursing-home operators under the MEDICAID program to be diverted from nursing-homes to help people with disabilities pay for personal attendants. Prior to the enactment of the ADA, ADAPT targeted the American Public Transit Association over the issue of accessible public transportation. Now, their target is the national nursing-home trade association the American Health Care Association (AHCA).

During the issue over accessible public transportation, ADAPT held protests in Cincinnati, St. Louis, Phoenix, Detroit, Atlanta, and Washington, D.C. In addition to picketing, the ADAPT protesters often locked their wheelchairs together in front of city buses or chained themselves to a bus bumper. On the nursing-home issue, the militant actions are directed towards Dr. Louis W. Sullivan, the Secretary of the Health and Human Services as well as towards the AHCA.

At the October 1991 AHCA Conference in Orlando, Florida, ADAPT blocked the entrances to the Peabody Hotel (the AHCA Conference hotel), and the Orange County (Orlando, Florida) Civic Center, the site of the Conference. After smashing their wheelchairs into police barricades and blocking the hotel's entrance, 73 of the ADAPT protesters were arrested.

Critics of ADAPT acknowledge that the burning images of people with physical disabilities (in wheelchairs) engaged in civil disobedience succeed in shattering the stereotyped image of a wheelchair user. When asked about the purpose of the blockade, ADAPT cofounder

Mike Auberger stated: "We want them to feel the inconvenience when they can't get where they want to go." The authors of this chapter can personally attest to the effectiveness of the ADAPT blockade at the AHCA Conference in Orlando. Both served as exhibitor/representatives for the National Library Service for the Blind and Physically Handicapped exhibit at the Conference.

**Sources**: "Wheelchair-bound Activists Block Hotel," Tallahassee *Democrat* (October 7,1991:2B) and "Militant Advocates for Disabled Revel in Their Role as Agitators," by Steven A. Holmes, New York *Times* (October 10, 1991:1C).

## SELECTED REFERENCES

American Civil Liberties Union, AIDS Project, ADA Education Project. 1991. *The Americans with Disabilities Act: What it means for people living with AIDS*. New York: ACLU Foundation.

Dana, John Cotton. 1902. Meaning of the public library in a city's life. *Library Journal*:755

Jarrow, Jane. 1991. Issues on campus and the road to ADA. *Educational Record* 72(Winter):26-31.

Kraus, Lewis E. and Susan Stoddard. 1989. *Chartbook on disabilities in the United States*. Washington, DC: National Institute on Disability and Rehabilitation.

Mahar, Mary Helen. 1982. Office of education support of school media programs. *Journal of Research and Development in Education* 16:19-25.

National Advisory Committee on the Handicapped. 1976. *The unfinished revolution: Education for the handicapped. 1976 annual report*. Washington, DC: GPO.

National Council on Disability. 1989. *The education of students with disabilities: Where do we stand. A report to the President and the Congress of the United States*. Washington, DC: National Council on Disability.

National Information Center for Children and Youth with Disabilities. 1991. The education of children and youth with special needs: What do the laws say? *News Digest* 1 (no. 1).

Needham, William L. and Gerald Jahoda. 1983. *Improving library service to physically disabled persons: A self-evaluation checklist*. Littleton, CO: Libraries Unlimited.

Peterson, Michael. 1989. Models of vocational assessment of handicapped students. *American Annals of the Deaf* 134 (October):273-276.

Rothstein, Laura F. 1990. *Special education law.* New York: Longman.

Thornburgh, Richard. 1991. A note from the attorney general. Introduction to *The Americans with Disabilities Act: Questions and answers.* Washington, DC: U.S. Department of Justice.

Trieschmann, Roberta B. 1987. *Aging with a disability.* New York: Demos.

Tucker, Bonnie P. 1989. Section 504 of the Rehabilitation Act after ten years of enforcement: The past and the future. *University of Illinois Law Review* 4:890.

U.S. Department of Education, Office of Special Education and Rehabilitative Services. 1991. *To assure the free appropriate public education of all children with disabilities: Thirteenth annual report to Congress on the implementation of Individuals with Disabilities Act.* Washington, DC: U.S. Department of Education.

U.S. General Services Administration et al. 1988. *Uniform federal accessibility standards.* Washington, DC:GPO.

Velleman, Ruth A. 1990. *Meeting the needs of people with disabilities: A guide for librarians, educators, and other service professionals.* Phoenix, AZ: Oryx Press.

Velleman, Ruth A. 1964. *School library service for physically handicapped children: An account of the library program at the Human Resources School, Albertson, NY.* Master's thesis, Palmer Graduate Library School, C. W. Post College of Long Island University. Quoted in Ruth A. Velleman. 1990. *Meeting the needs of people with disabilities: A guide for librarians, educators, and other service professionals.* Phoenix, AZ: Oryx Press.

Weintraub, Frederick J. and Bruce A. Ramirez. 1985. *Progress in the education of the handicapped and analysis of P.L. 98-199: The Education of the Handicapped Act Amendments of 1983.* Reston, VA: Council for Exceptional Children.

# APPENDIXES

# APPENDIX A
# How to Get the Americans with Disabilities Act and Its Regulations and Guidelines

The ADA and its regulations and guidelines are readily available in the *Federal Register* or without charge from the respective federal agencies as follows:

United States Congress, **Americans with Disabilities Act of 1990,** Public Law 101-336—July 26, 1990 (42 *USC* 12101-12213)(104 *STAT* 327-378). The Act to establish a clear and comprehensive prohibition of discrimination on the basis of disability was enacted by the 101st Congress of the Senate and House of Representatives of the United States. The Act contains five titles: Title I (Employment), Title II (Public Services), Title III (Public Accommodations and Services Operated by Private Entities), Title IV (Telecommunications), and Title V (Miscellaneous Provisions). Copies are available from the Office on the Americans with Disabilities Act, Civil Rights Division, U.S. Department of Justice, Post Office Box 66118, Washington, D.C. 20035-6118. Electronic bulletin board: (202) 514-6193; Voice: (202) 514-0301; TDD: (202) 514-0381 and (202) 514-0383. These are not toll-free numbers.

United States Architectural and Transportation Barriers Compliance Board, Part II (36 *CFR* Part 1191) **Americans with Disabilities Act (ADA) Accessibility Guidelines for Building and Facilities; Final Guidelines** (56 *Federal Register,* July 26, 1991):35408-35453. Appendix to Part 1191—**Accessibility Guidelines for Building and Facilities** is included in Part II. These final guidelines were issued to assist the U.S. Department of Justice to establish standards for new construction and alterations in places of public accommodation and commercial facilities, as required by Title III of the ADA. This document is available in accessible formats: cassette tape, Braille, large print, or computer disk upon request from the Office of the General Counsel, Architectural and Transportation Compliance Board, 1111-18th Street, NW, Suite 501, Washington, D.C. 20036. Telephone: (202) 653-7834 (Voice/TDD). This is not a toll-free number.

---

United States Department of Justice, Office of the Attorney General, Part III (28 *CFR* Part 36) **Nondiscrimination on the Basis of Disability by Public Accommodations and in Commercial Facilities; Final Rule** (56 *Federal Register*, July 26, 1991):35544-35691. This rule implements Title III of the ADA. It requires that all new places of public accommodation and commercial facilities be designed and constructed so as to be readily accessible to and usable by persons with disabilities, and requires that examinations or courses related to licensing or certification for professional and trade purposes be accessible to persons with disabilities. Copies of this rule are available in large print, Braille, electronic file on computer disk, and audiotape from the Office on the ADA at (202) 514-0301 (Voice) or (202) 514-0318 (TDD); and also available on electronic bulletin board at (202) 514-6193. These are not toll-free numbers.

---

United States Department of Justice, Office of the Attorney General, Part IV (28 *CFR* Part 35) **Nondiscrimination on the Basis of Disability in State and Local Government Services; Final Rule** (56 *Federal Register*, July 26, 1991): 35694-35723. This rule implements Subtitle A of Title II of ADA which prohibits discrimination on the basis of disability by public entities. It extends the prohibition of discrimination in federally assisted programs established by Section 504 of the Rehabilitation Act of 1973 to all activities of state and local governments, including those that do not receive federal assistance, and incorporates specific prohibitions of discrimination on the basis of disability from Title(s) I, III, and V of the ADA. Copies are available from the Office on the ADA, Civil Rights Division of the U.S. Department of Justice, Post Office Box 66118, Washington, D.C. 20035-6118. Electronic bulletin board: (202) 514-6193; Voice:

(202) 514-0301; TDD: (202) 514-0381 and (202) 514-0383. These are not toll-free numbers.

---

United States Equal Employment Opportunity Commission (EEOC), Part V (29 *CFR* Part 1630) **Equal Employment Opportunity for Individuals with Disabilities; Final Rule** and (29 *CFR* Part(s) 1602 and 1627) **Recordkeeping and Reporting Under Title VII of the Civil Rights Act of 1964** and the **Americans with Disabilities Act (ADA); Final Rule** (56 *Federal Register*, July 26, 1991):35726-35756. Section 106 of the ADA requires that the EEOC issue substantive regulations implementing Title I (Employment) within one year of the date of enactment of the Act. The EEOC issued new Part 1602 to its regulations to implement Title I and Sections 3(2), 3(3), 501, 503, 506(e), 508, 510, and 511 of the ADA as those sections pertaining to employment. New Part 1630 prohibits discrimination against qualified individuals with disabilities in all aspects of employment. Copies of this final rule and interpretive appendix may be obtained by calling the Office of Communications and Legislative Affairs at (202) 663-4900. Copies of this rule are available in large print, Braille, electronic file on computer disk, and audiotape from the EEOC by calling (202) 663-4398 or (202) 663-4395 (Voice) or (202) 663-4399 (TDD). These are not toll-free numbers.

## Appendix B
# Americans with Disabilities Act Statutory Deadlines

The statutory deadlines for the Americans with Disabilities Act of 1990 are as follows:

I. **Employment**
   The ADA requirements become effective on:
   > July 26, 1992, for employers with 25 or more employees
   >
   > July 26, 1994, for employers with 15-24 employees

II. **Public Accommodations**
   The ADA requirements become effective on:
   > January 26, 1992, generally
   >
   > August 26, 1990, for purchase or lease of new vehicles that are required to be accessible
   >
   > New facilities designed and constructed for first occupancy later than January 26, 1993, must be accessible

   Generally, lawsuits may not be filed until January 26, 1992. In addition, except with respect to new construction and alterations, no lawsuit may be filed until:
   > July 26, 1992, against businesses with 25 or fewer employees and gross receipts of $1 million or less
   >
   > January 26, 1993, against businesses with 10 or fewer employees and gross receipts of $500,000 or less

## III. Transportation

A. *Public bus systems*

The ADA requirements become effective on:

January 26, 1992, generally

August 26, 1990, for purchase or lease of new buses

B. *Public rail systems*—light, rapid, commuter, and intercity (Amtrak) rail

The ADA requirements become effective on:

January 26, 1992, generally

August 26, 1990, for purchase or lease of new rail vehicles

By July 26, 1995, one car per train accessibility must be achieved

By July 26, 1993, existing key stations in rapid, light, and commuter rail systems must be made accessible with extensions of up to 20 years (30 years, in some cases, for rapid and light rail)

C. *Privately operated bus and van companies*

The ADA requirements became effective on:

January 26, 1992, generally

January 26, 1996 (July 26, 1997, for small providers) for purchase of new over-the-road buses

August 26, 1990, for purchase or lease of certain new vehicles (other than over-the-road buses)

## IV. State and Local Government Operations

The ADA requirements become effective on:

January 26, 1992

## V. Telecommunications

The ADA requirements become effective on :

July 26, 1993, for provision of relay services.

For more information on the ADA, contact U.S. Department of Justice, Civil Rights Division, Coordination and Review Section, P.O. Box 66118, Washington, D.C. 20035-6118. Telephone: Voice: (202) 514-0301; TDD: (202) 514-0381 and (202) 514-0383. These are not toll-free numbers.

# APPENDIX C
# National Library Service for the Blind and Physically Handicapped

## Materials

A free material library service providing recorded (on disc and cassette) and Braille materials to blind and physically handicapped persons is administered by the National Library Service for the Blind and Physically Handicapped (NLS), a National Program in the Library of Congress. With the cooperation of authors and publishers who grant permission to use copyrighted works, NLS selects and produces full-length books and magazines in Braille and on recorded disc and cassette. The recording materials produced are then distributed to a cooperating network of regional and subregional libraries that circulate them to eligible borrowers in their respective service areas by postage-free mail. Forty-six regional and ninety-one subregional libraries are currently (1991) part of the network, serving all parts of the United States, Puerto Rico, the Virgin Islands, and Guam. Network libraries, in addition to the distribution of materials and equipment, also offer reference, reader's advisory, and other services.

## Eligible Borrowers

Eligible borrowers at all ages—children, young adult, and adult—may receive these services. Established by Congress in 1931 to serve blind adults, the program was expanded in 1952 to include children, and again in 1966 by Public Law 89-552 to include individuals with physical impairments that prevent the reading of standard print.

## Equipment

Playback equipment is loaned free for use with books and magazines recorded on disc and on cassette. Special accessories supplied on request include special amplifiers, remote control units, breath switches, extension levers, head-phones, and pillow-phones. Network libraries and other designated machine-lending agencies serve as distribution points for playback equipment and accessories.

## Applications

Applications for library service from eligible persons or institutions, such as nursing facilities, schools (elementary, secondary, and academic), public libraries, hospitals, agencies, and similar institutions are made directly to the network library serving a particular geographic area. Some network libraries provide deposit collections of materials and playback equipment to institutions within their respective service areas. Individual subscription services are also available from network libraries. Application forms, demonstration equipment, and sample reading materials are available in many local public libraries.

## Bibliography Center

The National Library Service functions as a bibliographic center on reading materials for people with disabilities and can make referrals to libraries and organizations that have materials in special media. Through its reference section, the NLS serves as a national information resource on various aspects of handicapping conditions. Music services are provided by the NLS Music Section, which has an extensive collection of music scores, books, and instructional materials in Braille, large print, and recorded media.

## Directory

On an annual basis, the National Library Service for the Blind and Physically Handicapped at the Library of Congress publishes a directory entitled *Library Resources for the Blind and Physically Handicapped: A Directory with FY [1992] Statistics on Readership Circulation, Budget, Staff, and Collections.* The information about NLS network libraries and machine-lending agencies contained in the body of the directory is provided by each network library and machine-lending agency in response to a NLS questionnaire circulated in February of the current year. Free copies of this directory are available to libraries and organizations by contacting: Reference Section, National Library Service for the Blind and Physically Handicapped, Library of Congress, Washington, D.C. 20542.

# APPENDIX D
# Other Disability Legislation Prior to the ADA

**Architectural Barriers Act of 1968:** Federal government buildings must be accessible to people with disabilities . . . compliance body established in 1973 was the Architectural and Transportation Barriers Compliance Board. Prompted formation of Uniform Accessiblity Standards.

---

**Rehabilitation Act (Sections 501 and 503) of 1973:** Requires affirmative action programs with goals, targeted disabilities, and advancement for people with disabilities in federal agencies and in federal government contracts.

---

**Rehabilitation Act (Section 504) of 1973:** Major conceptual foundation of the ADA. Section 504 (Discrimination under Federal Grants) prohibits discrimination against "otherwise qualified individuals with handicaps" in any program or activity receiving federal financial assistance.

---

**Education for All Handicapped Children Act of 1975:** Addresses primarily the exclusion of children with disabilities from public schools and inappropriate programs for many attending school.

**Developmental Disabilities Act of 1975**: Made federal grant money available to states which comply with certain procedures for care and treatment programs for people with severe or long-term disabilities occurring prior to age 22.

**Voting Accessibility Act of 1984**: Makes accessible all polling places and registration facilities for federal elections.

**Air Carrier Access Act of 1986**: Prohibits discrimination of people with disabilities by all air carriers.

**Fair Housing Amendments Act of 1989**: Expanded enforcement mechanisms of the Fair Housing Act, which prohibited discrimination in the sale or rental of private housing, to include people with disabilities.

**Americans with Disabilities Act of 1990**: Establishes a clear and comprehensive prohibition of discrimination on the basis of disability.

# Index

## BY JOAN GRIFFITTS